CONTENTS

A
COUNTRY
LIFE

A
COUNTRY
LIFE

At Home in the English Countryside

Roy Strong

St. Martin's Press ⚌ New York

Cover Illustration © Julia Trevelyan Oman. Published by arrangement with Transworld Publishers, a division of the Random House Group Ltd.

www.stmartins.com

Library of Congress Cataloging-in-Publication Data

Strong, Roy C.
    A country life : at home in the English countryside / Roy Strong.—
1st U.S. ed.
        p. cm.
    ISBN 0-312-30709-8
    1. Gardening—England—Herefordshire. 2. Strong, Roy C.—
Homes and haunts—England—Herefordshire. 3. Country life—
England—Herefordshire. 4. Country life (London, England).
    I. Title.

SB455 .S843 2003
635'.09424'4—dc21   2002031921

First published in Great Britain by Pavillion Books Limited.

First U.S. Edition: March 2003

10 9 8 7 6 5 4 3 2 1

For Beatrix
Best of Friends

PREFACE

THE majority of these pieces first appeared under 'Countryman's Week' in *Country Life* between 1989 and 1994. That they were written at all I owe to the former editor, Jenny Green, who asked me to contribute. As a consequence I found myself taking my writing in a novel direction, celebrating in effect what was a new phase of life after decades of public office. Judging from the letters I received, that occasional column must have struck a chord with people, which is why the articles have been gathered together here as a modest miscellany for a bedside browse. In so doing they have been arranged under season to make a single year, forming, I trust, a forgivable poetic fiction.

The scene, however, is set by an essay I wrote for *Hortus* in 1992. The description of our house, The Laskett, and its setting will enable the reader to get his bearings in our eccentric domain.

I am grateful to the present editor of *Country Life*, Clive Aslet, and to the editor of *Hortus* for allowing me to use material which first appeared under their auspices. I am even more grateful to my wife, Julia Trevelyan Oman, because it was she to whom I first read all these pieces, seeking her *imprimatur*. She it is who is the true muse of *A Country Life*.

Roy Strong
March 1994

THE LASKETT
A House in the Country

L ET me begin at the beginning. The Laskett, a word
in Herefordshire dialect meaning a strip of land
without the parish, lies on the fringes of the village
of Much Birch, mid-way between Ross-on-Wye and
Hereford. As my wife, Julia Trevelyan Oman, always
says, it is building rather than architecture, a pink sandstone box from the 1820s, evoking the modesty of a
rectory in a novel by Jane Austen.

The house itself has an undistinguished but pleasingly
symmetrical façade, three sash windows aloft and, below,
a jutting porch flanked by two later bay windows. As for
its interior, it was once characterized by my wife as
'work rooms with a few state apartments attached'. I
suppose that if I was asked to describe it, I would say that
it is an artist's house, full of decorative clutter arranged to
charm but not impress, and solidly based on the demands
of comfort. Like the garden, which spreads out from it,
everything in it is charged with memory, from a bowl of
pot-pourri to a postcard perched near the breakfast table.

Books are everywhere, spilling over from my small
library and writing room out along the landing and
through the guest bedrooms. Downstairs they wend their
way around the dining-room, on through the kitchen
into the garden room, and finally up and around a flight
of stairs into my wife's studio complex in the old stables.
Next to books, the interior is dominated by plants.
Everywhere one looks, geraniums and pelargoniums

climb and sprawl, with the addition in spring of bowls of hyacinths and 'Paper Whites'. Virtually no windowsill is devoid of containers and *cachepots*, the bay windows are transformed into bowers of ascending greenery and the conservatory is just plain stuffed, especially during the winter when the agapanthus are brought in.

So it is a house dominated by both books and plants, but even more by cats. Our two American Maine Coons, Larkin and Souci, are recent successors to the Reverend Wenceslas Muff and, before him, the Lady Torte de Shell. I am afraid that no door is too sacred not to have a hole cut through it to facilitate the passage of these glorious creatures. The kitchen is dominated by their commodious nests and subsidiary outposts are dotted throughout the house. The heart of the place is, however, the kitchen and the Aga. From that room everything fans outwards through doors that lead to scullery and studio, drawing room and conservatory, hall and breakfast room. It is an intimate house and, if I had to epitomize its atmosphere, I would have to resort to a foreign word, for in the main it is pure Biedermeier, the style of Shubert's Vienna, elegant, modest and reflecting a genuine delight in domestic life.

That a huge garden might be made there was certainly never part of our plan at the outset, as is reflected in the fact that no one who was going to make a large formal garden would ever have chosen a house sited, as ours is, in the corner of a three-and-a-half-acre triangle of land, thus eliminating any possibility of the classic progression through parterres, bosquets and walks radiating from and related to the house. But in the long run that deficiency has been found to have its advantages. The first is the one of surprise: nobody visiting the house and garden for the first time can ever guess at the spectacle that suddenly unfolds as they cross the drive past a fountain and through a slip in a beech hedge. Turning sharply left there is a great vista falling away into the distance, through three gardens, towards glimpses of a pleached lime avenue. That is where the garden proper begins.

To a sense of surprise I would add the ability to indulge in certain grand effects which, if sited in proximity to the house, would have appeared too pretentious and out of place. The ten-foot-high column topped by a golden ball, the nine-foot-high Shakespeare Urn (commemorating the award to me in 1980 of the FVS Foundation of Hamburg's Shakespeare Prize), and the small classical Victoria & Albert temple (built in memory of the years 1974 to 1987), which make up the eyecatchers at the ends of the grandest vistas, are so far from the house that they have taken on the character of total fantasies in an imaginary land-scape.

Both house and garden are

south-facing and the land gently slopes away, presenting us at the outset with few level surfaces except that of the site of an Edwardian lawn-tennis court. And that was where we started. It was in a field attached to the house, and let to a farmer as pasture for his cows. His decision in 1974 to stop renting the field set us on our way. Together we stood and looked at the three-foot-high grass and realized that something had to be done; and it was on the flat surface of the court, when mowing had revealed the fine turf beneath the grass, that we began, in the December of that year, to plant one of our first yew hedges, around what was to be the Pierpont Morgan Rose Garden. At the time I felt a lack of flat terrain a tremendous disadvantage, but now I realize our good fortune, as changes in level, as every true gardener knows, form some of the most thrilling experiences. That only dawned much later, when we learned that built structure could be added as and when it could be afforded. So, piecemeal over the years, the flights of steps and paving came, necessitating only a realignment of hedges, letting one side grow up to re-establish levels within the composition.

But what about the soil? It is light and sandy, reddish in colour, too quick-draining and calling for constant compost and mulch to keep the moisture in. It tolerates rhododendrons and azaleas but they cannot be said exactly to thrive. Willows will not grow, and all except the most common of prunus are fated. Putting those black marks aside, practically everything else does pretty well and some things spectacularly so. Yew hedging, one of my great loves, shoots up at the rate of a foot to eighteen inches a year and, as most of the garden's most important rooms are formed of it, this has proved a great blessing. Sprigs two feet high become eight-foot walls in a decade. And, of course, Herefordshire being a cider county, malus flourish, and my wife's passion has become old apple trees and the decorative crabs, of which altogether she now has some hundred or so. This soil is also an ideal one in which to grow grey foliage plants but, as they are tender, one has to protect them from the wind.

Wind, in fact, even more than rabbits and moles, was to be and still is our greatest enemy; horrendous gales blowing from the Black Mountains, felling branches, even whole trees. The garden's climatic history has included the great drought of 1976 and the bitter winters of the early 1980s; in one of those we suffered from 24 degrees of frost which wiped out much, including a fifteen-foot-high avenue of New Zealand beech.

To these minuses we can add that on arrival we had to take down seven dead elm trees, and that the chestnut avenue up the drive promptly died, to be followed a few years after by a superb beech and a turkey oak. None the less, an ever-open cheque book and a succession of tree surgeons have ensured that the mighty cedar of Lebanon which holds the whole house in its arms still presides over the front lawn.

But I have yet to explain what led us to do it, apart from the necessity of filling the field with something. 1974 was my first year as Director of the Victoria & Albert Museum. It was the period of the fall of the Heath government, the oil crisis, and industrial and social unrest. The feeling of uncertainty about the future of things was encapsulated in the first exhibition I and my team rushed into the museum, *The Destruction of the Country House*. This brought home to the public, by using the museum as polemic, the full horror of what we had lost in this century, in terms not only of houses but of gardens, too, and went on to spell out the dangers ahead. It was a time of deep gloom, and I clearly remember that the act of planting that garden was a deliberate and defiant one. In spite of all, I believed with a great passion that the most English of all art forms, the classic country house garden, would go on. With no money, little labour, but much love and not a little vision, we would make one. We would plant our yews in this dark hour, and hold fast in the knowledge that they would grow and that we would live to clip them into pinnacles and peacocks; and so it has proved. But that could not be foreseen amid the turbulence of the second half of the 1970s.

By 1975 we had a plan; in fact I still have what I drew in the summer of that year. Its design emerged out of what I loved and knew best. There was never any question but that the garden was to be formal. Indeed, I was mesmerized by the country house views in Kip's *Nouveau Théâtre de la Grande Bretagne*, recording late Stuart gardens with their stately avenues, pattern planting and enclosures. It also struck me as being a not particularly labour-intensive form of gardening, for it gave architecture and articulation purely through the ordered siting of trees and shrubs, some of which would only call for an annual prune or clip. Next for inspiration came the photographs by Charles Latham in *Gardens Old and New* (1910), that set of volumes which records the country house gardens of Edwardian England on the eve of the deluge of 1914. Constantly I would go for walks in those photographs, looking for ideas for The Laskett – ideas, that is, that we could afford.

Then there were the real gardens. Hidcote Manor, of course, first visited by us on a chill winter's day with the late Lady Hartwell. Pamela's husband Michael has made a marvellous garden of this kind at Oving, which was another inspiration because it consisted purely of trees and shrubs held together by sculptural ornament. Two other friends provided further impulses: Sir Cecil Beaton and John Fowler. Cecil was actually the first person ever to walk me round a garden, which he regularly did at his house in Reddish. This seemingly simple act, like so many in one's life, was seminal in opening up to me the very idea that one could actually make a garden at all. Although Beaton's garden was beautiful, its design never affected me as much as John Fowler's miraculous creation at King John's Hunting Lodge at Odiham in Hampshire. This is the most perfectly articulated small garden I have ever seen. It excited me above all as to the effects which could be achieved by training. Features such as the stilt hedges and the use of clipped box for formal accents stayed imprinted on my mind.

The trouble is that, almost twenty years on, so many other influences have come tumbling in. Italy certainly, which I first fell in love with in 1955, but the gardens only came in the 1970s. The Villa Lante or the Villa Farnese haunted me; it was fifteen years before we could afford to grace the first grand vista with steps, balustrading and a distant temple, but such artefacts were always in my mind's eye from the very beginning. William III's palace of Het Loo, that supreme restoration of a late seventeenth-century garden in Holland, constantly seized my imagination during the 1980s, with the result that more box and ground patterns began to spring up everywhere. The Yew Garden near the house, where I planted my first minute box parterre, suddenly exploded in size. A box and gravel parterre with our initials entwined at its centre was laid out on the far side of the garden and, in front of the house, a design from John Marriott's *Knots for Gardens* (1618) was planted, adding a carpet at the feet of a statue of Flora.

The main layout of the garden has never really radically changed over two decades, but it has been developed and refined enormously. This is not only the result of having seen new things, but also of having made terrible mistakes, or of finding that a particular scheme was either unmaintainable or simply did not work. Garden ornaments in particular have frequently migrated before finding their final resting-place. Over ornament, I have no snobbery, and ours is a happy mish-mash of old and new; in fact, whatever I think I can get away with at a distance. I would like to have new things, and perhaps we shall achieve that one day. The Associates of the Victoria & Albert Museum presented me with our only new artefact as a farewell present, a plaque by Simon Verity, which is like a medal, in which my profile is sandwiched between that of the Queen and the Prince Consort.

The achievement of any garden must be considered in

relation to the commitment in terms of both time and labour. Contrary to general belief, formality and size are marvellous concealers of untidiness and lack of finish. Through the fourteen years that I directed the museum, I was never able to give the garden the input it demanded. But it was during these very years that its vital infrastructure of shrubberies, hedges and screens grew, making the later elaboration possible. All of this has been achieved by just the two of us, plus the equivalent of an untrained gardener one day a week. We had to accept a relaxed philosophy over what got done and what had to be left. If the weeds sprang and the branches got entangled, we merely looked at those areas through romantic eyes. Now for the first time we have help in the garden for four days a week, and cannot contain our excitement as to what we hope to achieve in this new era.

Inevitably, plants have until recently had to take

something of a back seat. One of the great joys of this present phase is to see that position being slowly reversed. In 1988 I planted a Flower Garden; it is rather Reptonesque in shape, but for the first time I was able to indulge in and learn about herbaceous borders, and start thinking more intensively about the season sequences. The Silver Jubilee Garden, once only at its apogee in a froth of white and lilac in June, now has an autumn finale of Michaelmas daisies coinciding with the second flush of the 'Iceberg' roses. Julia has turned her hand to the spring planting, which now unfolds in a complex rhythm which begins in January and lasts until the close of May. Flora in her glade is never without a bloom at her feet from the earliest snowdrops, through aconites, scillas, chionodoxas, tiny daffodils, and fritillaries. The formal beds are planted in succession to achieve a display of tulips and hyacinths over as long a period as possible. The stunning great *allée* of daffodils along the pleached lime avenue is succeeded by purple alliums amid cow parsley, like a Sisley painting. The winding walk, the Serpentine, is thick with ribbons of 'White Lion' daffodils, which fade as the Flower Garden springs to life. Recent new planting at the boundaries is aimed at giving glorious sunset-coloured foliage to enliven the autumn skyline. And this year Julia has transformed yet another area to take her collection of snowdrops and irises in raised beds. The greatest excitement, in terms of summer planting, has been in the Fountain Court, now entering its second year, the grey foliage plants already cooling the weathered brick paths and the specie roses about to take off, echoing the explosion of the fountain jet but this time with a cascade of pink and white blooms.

The Laskett is an autobiographical garden, for our life together is etched into its many compartments. They have to be named, and often they were constructed with money made through a book or a theatrical production. It must sound eccentric to visitors as they are guided through the Pierpont Morgan Rose Garden (I gave the Walls Lectures there in 1974), along the pleached lime avenue, Elizabeth Tudor (my wife and I did a book on her in 1972), or sit in the Ashton Arbour of clipped yew (named to recall Sir Frederick, two of whose ballets Julia designed), looking towards a tableau of topiary peacocks set, as it were, on a stage which we call Covent Garden (where Julia also designed three operas). It is all a bit arbitrary and sometimes, in the case of the statuary, just plain dotty. A recumbent stag will be christened Franco because of a book I wrote for the brilliant Italian publisher Franco Maria Ricci, or a classical female bust Lucia because we were in an E. F. Benson phase.

But it does mean that every space in the garden is thick with association and memories of a life together, and of our mutual creativity. Of course, it is rich beyond that with other memories, above all of people. A sundial from Cecil Beaton's garden stands at the centre of the garden we planted in honour of the Queen's Silver Jubilee in 1977. That to me symbolizes a precious friendship, for I often stayed with him, and the exhibition of his portrait photographs at the National Portrait Gallery in 1968 lit the blue touchpaper of my career. Julia's family, the Omans, is recalled by an urn at the centre of the Rose Garden, which came from her aunt, the writer Carola Oman's house at Bride Hall in Hertfordshire. A pinnacle from All Souls and a lion from the Houses of Parliament are evidence of her distinguished grandfather, Sir Charles Oman, the historian and MP for the University of Oxford. These came from Frewin Hall where he lived, as also did a descendant of a quince tree which now flourishes at The Laskett, and the agapanthus which have multiplied and been passed down through the family for almost a century. Every year we look forward to that heavenly blue bursting upon us on the terrace.

I have not yet mentioned either the orchard or the vegetable garden, which are my wife's domain. Apple trees are her obsession, and we have over sixty varieties, going back to the twelfth century, all of them on dwarf rooting stock. They look beautiful in spring with their explosion of bloom, and equally ravishing in autumn laden with fruits. A Finnish apple steamer bubbles away during the fruiting season, producing juice which we bottle and lay down. A second, smaller orchard contains peaches, and in a good year can produce up to thirty. But it is the vegetable garden that is our real cornucopia. It makes no claim to be a decorative potager, although it has at its centre a small arched tunnel heavy with honeysuckle, an 'Albertine' rose, and what the friend who gave it to me calls the 'Gardener's Rose'. Spilling over amid the vegetables will be pot marigolds, nasturtiums and hardy geraniums, and herbs of every kind. But it is the edible produce which is its heart. Joy Larkcom's oriental vegetables have given it a new dimension, but we also always purchase seeds in France and Italy and cast them upon the earth in hope. The fact that for ten months of the year we eat our own salad greens is some measure of the success. There are asparagus, onions, potatoes, carrots, leeks, spinach, as well as gooseberries, Jerusalem artichokes and rhubarb. Beyond this wired enclosure about a dozen compost heaps are dotted, many held down by black plastic sheeting with rubber car tyres, monuments to the impact of our visit to the compost queen of Dieppe, Princess Sturdza, who manages to transform beech leaves into black soot with the wave of her hand, in only six weeks.

Rosemary Verey, to whose encouragement we owe so much, once wrote that The Laskett is the largest formal garden in England to be planted from scratch since 1945. I wonder. If you asked me what The Laskett garden was about, I might reply that it is the portrait of a marriage, the family we never had (or wanted), a unique mnemonic landscape peopled with the ghosts of nearly everyone we have loved, both living and dead. It has always been conceived as an enclosed private world, and that indeed is the key. There is no borrowed landscape. It deliberately shuts out the glory of the rolling hills of Herefordshire and remains a sealed, hermetic, magical domain of its own. And yet there is never a sense of being shut in, of claustrophobia. Just one of serene tranquillity, or as much of it as can be granted in this transitory life. For me its making has been a more extraordinary achievement than any of the books I have written or museums I have directed. To take a basket with two glasses and a bottle of wine up to the Victoria & Albert Temple on a summer's evening, and sit contemplating the vista together in silence, is happiness quantified. What more can one ask?

KEY TO PLAN

1 House	16 Tatiana's Walk
2 Glyndebourne	17 Silver Jubilee
3 The Canal	Garden
4 Terrace	18 Pierpont Morgan
5 Yew Garden	Rose Garden
6 Torte's Garden	19 Sir Muff's Parade
7 Service Area	20 Scandinavian
8 Fledermaus Walk	Grove
9 Spring Garden	21 Elizabeth Tudor
10 The Glade and	(Pleached Lime
Flora	Avenue)
11 Knot Garden	22 The Serpentine
12 Fountain Court	23 Flower Garden
13 The Drive	24 The Hilliard
14 Small Orchard	Garden
15 Schönbrunn	25 Roy's Birthday
Orchard	Garden

26 The Beaton Steps
27 Shakespeare Urn
28 Hearne's Oak
29 Winter Rose
Walk
30 Ashton Arbour
31 Mary Queen of
Scots Walk
32 Covent Garden
33 Victoria &
Albert Temple
34 The Nutcracker
Garden
35 Christmas
Orchard
36 Gothick Arbour
37 Kitchen Garden

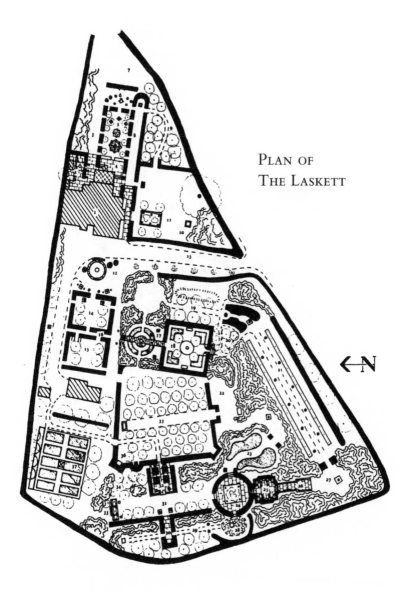

PLAN OF
THE LASKETT

←N

Plan by Simon Dorrell

SPRING

SPRING as a season is odd man out, for it can come early or late, with a rush or a whimper. Nor is it helped by Easter being a moveable feast ranging through late March to the close of April. Spring's harbingers are January's hellebores and snowdrops, hints and hopes of what is to come. At The Laskett I know that spring is really here when the pleached lime avenue we call Elizabeth Tudor is thick carpeted with daffodils, and that it has gone when the tulips in the Yew Garden close to the house wilt. It has arrived, too, when I can wander up to the kitchen garden and pick the first sprigs of tarragon, and also when the fountain, emptied for the duration of the winter, spurts and sparkles once again in the light outside the breakfast room window.

Hibernation stops. Layers of clothes begin to be shed. On the beds the duvets give way to sheets and blankets. Lunch ceases to call for hot soup. The stored vegetables from the previous year begin to run out and there is that awful in-between period before the new season's produce can begin to be harvested. One of the great excitements is the first mow of the year, re-establishing order on a nature which, in the coming months, will be all too rampant. Easter Day, however, provides the ultimate tableau. Out of a drawer in the cabinet, which also holds the Christmas decorations, comes a kaleidoscope of eggs to adorn the table: garish ones from Poland, wooden ones from India, sugar ones from sweet shops everywhere, even ones like plastic ping-pong balls.

Dyed, painted, stencilled, beribboned, each has a story to tell, but collectively they spell spring.

RUSTLE OF SPRING

❧❀❧

STATUESQUE Flora begins to scatter her cornucopia in January. She presides over the glade which encompasses the great cedar in front of the house, on which I look down from my writing room window. Suddenly, her basket filled with stone flowers takes on a reality, when my eagle eye spots a fleck of gold beneath – a solitary hoop-petticoat narcissus – the harbinger of successive tides of spring flowers which will carry on appearing until the end of April.

At the moment, the snowdrops are out, and so are groups of pale violet scillas, which seem to froth up through the grass, and the tiny daffodil 'Tête-à-Tête', with its rich, buttery yellows and ochres.

All memories of the backache that I gave myself planting them subside in the bliss of floral fulfilment. They beckon me out to examine them more closely, and then urge me on to search for other jewels – for early spring flowers somehow have to be suddenly alighted upon, or discovered. They are almost invariably small in scale – *pace* the hellebores – which emphasizes their preciosity, and they nestle, semi-hidden, in shady drifts beneath shrubs and trees, or are tucked into corners. It is the garden in its pointillist period, enlivened by myriad dots of colour; a preface to the Impressionist one that follows, with the onrush of daffodils and narcissi, and, above all, the blossom in the orchard. It is a journey that takes one from Seurat to Pissarro.

TRANSFORMATION SCENES

∾∿∿∾

HOAR frosts are the real glory of a snow-bereft winter. Frost sometimes only touches the landscape, etching it with silver, but a good hard hoar frost eclipses all, spangling every tree from tip to toe. A hazard for car windscreens, I must concede, as the sun's rays melt chunks of ice which thud onto its fragile surface. But that in no way diminishes the excitement of coursing along country roads transformed into a transitory sugared paradise.

At least three times since Christmas we have awoken to peer out of the bedroom window and be greeted by such enchantment. Unashamedly I respond to the intense theatricality of such frosts, for my reaction is inevitably bred of childhood memories of pantomime tranformation scenes or the snowflake sequence in *The Nutcracker* ballet – old-fashioned stage spectacles in which spangled cut cloths and gauzes still weave their spell.

It can be no coincidence that scenes such as this first appeared on stage during a period notable for its extremes of cold – that of Restoration England, when the Thames froze over, to provide an arena for the famous frost fairs of which Pepys paints such memorable pictures. Theatre scenery, together with Dutch genre paintings of happy skaters disporting themselves on frozen canals, have certainly contributed to endowing frost with a romance belying its true nature.

RABBIT HOLOCAUST

༄༅༅༄

'RING Mac,' my wife occasionally says on returning from a garden tour, 'there's another one.' Julia is referring to some luckless rabbit that has been caught in a cage. If Mac, who is pest control, cannot come at once, the poor creature gets fed with pieces of carrot, unaware that he is the recipient of meals in the condemned cell.

Neither of us has the guts to go out and kill the animal, so there it sits until the executioner arrives. The corpse is gutted and hung near the back door, awaiting skinning and the deep freeze. Occasionally, we are told that it was pregnant and that we have wiped out five rabbits instead of one.

This is one episode in an ongoing saga to clear the garden of rabbits. Although we certainly have our own, the fields adjacent are also populated, yet the farmer who owns them says he has none. Perhaps I am having an hallucination every time I see them hopping around but, no matter, a rabbit fence would solve all – or so I thought.

At some cost, and not without dramas, the fence has been installed, creating a kind of rabbit island. But it is one thing to do that, and quite another to eliminate the rabbits from inside it, particularly as our own priority is the safety of our cat, the Reverend Wenceslas. So poison was out. Shooting at dusk involved keeping the cat indoors, and in any case, the result was only some three corpses. We are now into about month five of the rabbit saga, with clearly a long way to go.

On the plus side, however, rabbits are food for the pot. I always remember, when we stayed one January in a villa in Tuscany, almost twenty years ago, how the housekeeper would cook rabbit, wrapping it in the herbs she had plucked on her way in. So I turned to Wilma Pezzini's *The Tuscan Cookbook* and found, as I had hoped, succulent, earthy peasant dishes of the kind that fill the kitchen with the heady aroma that only a mixture of wine, oil, garlic, onions and tomatoes can produce.

Bored Cat

∾∾

Mention of domestic animals brings me to how inimical stormy weather is to them. The Reverend Wenceslas Muff sits in a mound in front of the Aga, bored. He is not asleep, for his ears twitch and his head and green eyes swivel round. Occasionally, he disappears outside, only to return rather fast with wet paws and his hair blown all over the place. He then proceeds to tidy himself up and resumes his immutable position.

Sometimes he goes to the back garden door, which is glass panelled, and just sits looking out, hoping for a break in the awful weather so that he can resume his normal life, inspecting fixed points on his map of the grounds, with tail horizontal and eyes and nose composed in lethal concentration. Let us hope that meteorological calm will return in time for his annual cull of the young rabbits.

SNOW FRIENDS

❦❧

IT is amazing how much clearing up there is to be
done in the weeks that see winter turning into spring,
particularly during a long winter that has brought snow.
Then, for instance, the bales of bubble plastic which my
wife assiduously stores from parcels and puts to use to
insulate any vulnerable parts of the house – swagged
across windows or pressed into apertures – have to be
folded and returned to store.

Snow is always a signal for a renaissance of camaraderie: 'Just ringing to see whether you're all right.' What everyone did before the telephone I don't know. A clerical friend of mine told me that at one of the more avant-garde Anglican churches they all have to hold hands around the altar and thank God for something. Snow comes high on the list for restoring the brotherhood of man.

On the day I was booked to lecture in aid of the National Art-Collections Fund in Cheltenham, I watched the flakes whirl past my writing room window, and received almost hourly reports. First my chauffeur was snowed in at Stanton. Then half the audience was cut off on the other side of the city.

By afternoon the event was off, and the splendid organizer was faced with a few hundred smoked salmon canapés minus the mouths to consume them. The wine, mercifully, could be returned unopened. Satisfactorily, the money could not be, so this non-event in the end achieved its purpose.

WRIGHT OF DERBY

∾⟁∾

EVERY minute that I am in London I ache for the country, and the Wright of Derby exhibition at the Tate Gallery transported me into the country, albeit to the north. I had forgotten what a wonderful painter he was of the English landscape, in which he so often places his north country businessmen and industrialists.

There was the marvellous pair of portraits of the

Milner brothers, sons of a cotton manufacturer, each standing beneath a venerable oak of the type which was to provide ships for Nelson's navy. Wright loved to catch the green leaves just on the turn, their edges barely tipped with gold, giving the whole picture a golden luminosity which reminded me of Cuyp.

His married friends he painted with a robust honesty and a kind of blissful happiness which bathes the parkland around them. Mr Coltman rests his arm on his wife's scarlet riding habit, she bending in profile towards him from her horse. Here the sense of impending autumn is even more intense, the foliage being almost ochre.

The Reverend Thomas Gisborne and his wife, born do-gooders, sit in their grounds beneath a huge sunshade. This time it is her turn to lean on him. Neither is handsome. She has a plain amiability, her dishevelled hair tied up with a scarf, giving her a chic one feels it certainly did not have.

There were walks to go on through the Derbyshire Peaks, with their cool light, and the Lakes looking like the Roman Campagna in canvas after canvas. And country dogs everywhere, a spaniel being hugged by children, fluffy terriers looking up sadly at their mistresses, and honest hunting hounds jumping up or just leaning a head on a sitter's knee in hope of attention.

A GREAT ECCENTRIC RECALLED

BUTTER-COLOURED aconites dapple the banks where once there stood a handsome beech tree at the top of the drive. When they appear I recall with a smile the great eccentric who gave them to us.

Lady (Charlotte) Bonham-Carter was never a peer's daughter, but was always Lady Charlotte to everyone. She was one of those rare people who seldom live at any time other than in the present. For decades she assumed the status of an institution in the London art world. She went everywhere: private views, parties, opera, ballet, concerts. Every occasion was grist to her mill, and her greatest determination was to miss nothing.

Until well into her nineties, every evening became a series of hors d'oeuvres with a bit of this and a bit of that. Starting off at a party, she would then tuck in a private view, pop up in a box at Covent Garden for act two of something, and no doubt move on for a finale elsewhere. She met the sartorial demands of this gypsy-like existence by rearranging a weird assortment of scarfs and shawls – an operation usually carried out behind a pillar or bush between events.

Stories about her are legion, for she had every quality that endears. She was a life-giver, never complaining and always generous. It did not matter how ghastly something was, she would lift up her lizard-like face and exclaim, 'My dear, wasn't that marvellous?' and somehow she made it so. Her great tragedy was failing to make her centenary by just two years.

Every year she held 'aconite parties' at her house in the country, where there were swathes. We never got to a party, but one day a cardboard box stuffed with plants wrapped in newspapers arrived in my office. It was the aconites. Now they nestle on the bank, quietly multiplying as the years pass, greeting us every time we arrive at the house. 'My dear, isn't that marvellous?' I feel, instinctively, she would have said.

A GOOD USE FOR NEWSPAPERS

∽∾∽

EVERY Christmas my wife gives me a *Cats in Art* diary whose function it is to act, for the most part, as a garden diary. The first thing I do is to transcribe from the previous year the major jobs to be done, either by our part-time gardeners, David and Wilf, or by ourselves. Apart from planting potatoes and onions, April contains two annotations in capital letters which read, 'Fertilizer on most things' and, under the last week, the fatal, 'Start spraying roses'.

The former for me, in the main, means an abundance of bonemeal on the yew hedges and, more particularly, the box hedging in the rose garden, which is now entering its third year. With a bit of luck, it might actually join up and establish at a glance the ordered geometry I want to achieve, containing within its walls what is, in effect, a mixed planting of roses and grey foliage plants.

Now this has changed. My wife has become obsessed with manufacturing compost heaps. Five stretch out in a row along one side of our vegetable garden, all in various stages of decomposition. Literally nothing escapes her acquisitive fingers, from kitchen peelings to newspapers. I can hardly put *The Times* or the *Independent* down before it is whisked away.

Recently, one of these magisterial heaps has, after several years, come to maturity and, thanks to David's shredder, I am blessed with rich compost for the flowerbeds. No matter how hard one tries, something inevitably gets into those heaps that should not, so I always have a bag to hand into which to pop the scraps of plastic and metal that I fish out as I fork the stuff around the plants. There is something enormously satisfying, aesthetically, in seeing the new green leaves and spring flowers against that dark, rich colour.

LENT LILIES

∾⚬⚬∾

EVEN by Quinquagesima we had spotted the first flush of those most enchanting of wildflowers, the daffodils we know as Lent lilies. Now they are in abundance. That early glimpse was along the M50 motorway leading to Ross-on-Wye, a road cut through a swathe of country which must once have been rich in fields dappled with them. Every so often from the car we would spot a field virtually carpeted, or the eye would dip to see a winding brook in a ravine whose banks were overhung with pools of pale creamy yellow flowerheads swaying in the breeze.

We had been told that the village of Dymock, just within the county of Herefordshire from Gloucestershire, was famed for the abundance of its Lent lilies. It was a frustrating expedition, made maddening by the fact that, as so often happens these days, some idiot had rotated the signpost to Dymock half circle. So we came first to

Upton Bishop, set on a hill, with the valley before it spread towards Ross.

Dymock, when we eventually found it, had a hidden lime walk leading from its handsome church in a gentle curve behind the houses, through a narrow lane between them, flanked by ancient box, and then out into the main street. This was some old footpath to the church that someone, sometime, had thought to enhance with this grand avenue. And there, on either side of it, were the lilies we sought.

JETSET

SPRING means turning the fountain on, an event that can develop the lunatic repercussions felt by Jacques Tati in *Mon Oncle*, in which there is the memorable sequence of him having to do precisely that every time someone rings the front door bell. Mercifully, our fountain goes on in spring and off with the first appearance of a severe frost, the basin being then emptied and the pump wrapped up for the winter. For months we stare out of the breakfast room window at this formidable ten-foot-high compilation of scrolls, masks, ascending water basins and crowning pineapple, sadly lifeless. Once we failed to empty the fountain in time and the frost came, but it did look glorious: huge, glistening stalactites of ice catching the morning sun. It cannot have done the object any good, but no matter.

This year the hard frosts were over towards the end of March and so the hose was run out to fill the basin, an operation that takes about five hours. Then I put the pump switch on in the kitchen and we stared out, hopefully. It never works first time. We always have to wallop the pump to dispel an airlock, but then the magic moment comes. Up through the central pineapple percolates first a dribble, then a splash and, finally, a soaring jet. Soon the smaller basins are full and water starts cascading downwards from one to the next. A shaft of spring sunshine on this tableau brings a sparkle and we know that spring is here.

OSBORNE REVISITED

I HAD not been to Osborne House, Queen Victoria's holiday villa on the Isle of Wight, for twenty years, and had quite forgotten what a time capsule it was. We went on a dull, lustreless day whose mist and incipient rain served only to heighten its mystery, causing one to view it as though through a theatrical gauze. It seemed like a huge set awaiting some new Visconti to people it.

There it stood, virtually unchanged since the 1850s and 60s, with its Italianate façades and arcaded galleries, its descending terraces, fountains and sculptured decoration. Every other moment it composed into an angle one remembered from a contemporary photograph or watercolour, onto which one superimposed with the mind's eye the missing crinolined figures clutching their parasols and the overdressed children.

Here was pseudo High Renaissance architecture rushed together in stucco over brick. The balustrading and urns, too, were cast composition and not stone, made by ancestors of the manufacturers of such things today, who, frankly, are better at it. Many of the garden statues are of bronzed zinc, and those of real bronze looked ill-at-ease on their common concrete plinths. We found ourselves wandering amid an amalgam of the Prince Consort's Italian memories, recast for the comfort of a later century in terms of the synthetic and the multiple.

I was struck by how much closer Osborne was to George IV's pavilion at Brighton than at first glance one would have guessed, and how Ludwig of Bavaria was really only just round the corner. I could not help thinking, too, how horrified Victoria and Albert would have been at being placed in such a line of descent.

Snowdrop Bequest

THE daffodils are now well and truly with us, but this year will be memorable more for the snowdrops which have never been so stunning. In addition to those that are scattered through the grounds, my wife has a collection of them housed in a raised bed held in by railway sleepers in the kitchen garden.

These were the gift a few years ago from an old gentleman whose cottage garden we visited. He was then well over eighty and anxious to pass on his precious heritage to caring hands – and in this he has succeeded. They are all in order, each with its own label, and now, to our great joy, multiplying.

Every year their shining whiteness brings to mind this gentle donor who opened his heart to us while we strolled around his garden, for he had recently been widowed. Not long afterwards he himself died, and we realized the true depth of his gesture, and how a fleeting friendship can in fact often deepen when the person is no longer there.

BURIED TREASURE

'I've found the 1920s domestic rubbish tip,' my wife exclaimed, holding up what looked like a small, long-necked glass vase which had, embossed on its bottom, 'Butler's Pommade Divine'. 'This is an original container,' I was told, as she proceeded to dilate at some length upon her memories of its miraculous healing properties. It seemed it was the mainstay of any decently run nursery first-aid cupboard, always ready to hand to cope with childish sores, chaps and bruises. In my medicinal mythology it runs neck and neck with Dr Collis Brown's chlorodyne, which is still available in its Victorian packaging and remains an essential component of any travelling kit. Pommade Divine, in this sense, has fared less well, and the last time we spotted it was in an old-fashioned chemist's in Bond Street, now gone. By then its container sadly had become plastic.

But to return to the domestic tip. This, in fact, is one of several which we have hit on over the years. All the pottery fragments – I would not have the effrontery to call them shards – get consigned to a cardboard box, with the idea that one day we shall make some sort of mosaic with them. I am amazed by how far-flung these tips can be, ranging to the furthest point of what we call the field, but which is now garden. In goes the fork and up comes another scattering of blue and white Victorian china, and odd fragments of hand-blown glass bottles. It is curious the fervour of speculative interest that these pieces of one's own humble domestic archaeology arouse, whereas I scoot past museum showcases loaded with the wonders of Aida's rubbish tip as fast as my legs can carry me.

THE RIGHT STUFF

GOOD craftsmen are rare, and we were fortunate to strike gold with some local upholsterers. There is a ritual to be gone through with these craftsmen, beginning with one of them coming to the house, neatly dressed in a dark suit and tie. The pieces in question would be inspected with an expert eye. There would be an inaudible hum of contentment at the thought of working on an eighteenth- or nineteenth-century chair or sofa. Bad workmanship they abhorred. Once I had two modern chairs back from them, together with some of what they had removed from the interiors, to show me the decline in workmanship.

But the great treat was to go to their workshop in Hereford. This was in a commodious, light room over a shop. Here the partners appeared, this time wearing spotless white aprons. Everything in sight was in good order, and I was taken up to the attic to view what awaited their attention – a dismal assembly, for the most part, of 1930s settees, post-war three-piece suites, together with the odd Victorian armchair and sofa. But what struck me most was that I had rarely seen such unmitigated filth, for the items were not just worn, the fabrics on them were torn, threadbare, many ripped to ribbons, and most caked with grime. I pondered how the magic of good craftsmanship was to transform these beyond recognition.

It reminded me of a story about a cousin of my wife's who was summoned to the upholsterers to see what had lain concealed in what the family had sat upon for the past few decades. There, sewn into the stuffing, was a Victorian workman's untouched lunch, tied in a handkerchief.

ODD MAN OUT

ంఠౖం

FEW things are more maddening in the gardening year than discovering that a solitary vibrant red tulip has crept into the middle of a bed of orange and white ones. But when one thinks of the huge scale of the bulb industry it is hardly surprising.

Charitable thoughts, however, are not the first to cross one's mind on spotting such an aberration, usually from the bedroom window and also at a time when, for one reason or another, one cannot get out. When at last one can, convulsed with aesthetic anguish, one descends on the poor flower like Conan the Barbarian.

This is the fault of the supplier, but just as irritating are one's own gaffes, as, however thorough one is in lifting the previous year's planting, one or two always escape the fork. Remnants of a previous colour scheme then surface to disfigure the new one or, even worse, push up through an area now put down to lawn. Perhaps one should not be so zealous, for these bulb disasters are as nothing compared with the hundreds of fritillaries planted in return, if we are lucky, for a handful of flowers.

FISHING

'HELLO Betty, are you joining the queue?' Betty, a grey-haired country woman in her late sixties, nodded assent. The queue in question forms every Thursday morning in Ross-on-Wye for fish. A bas-relief of the Man of Ross, John Kyrle, looks down approvingly from the red sandstone market house as we stand in line to be served.

All sorts and conditions of people who know when they are on to a good thing patiently wait. A source of really fresh fish is a perpetual battle for the inland country dweller. There are the supermarkets, of course, with their so-called fresh-fish counters and freezers awash with the stuff, but none of them touch this modest mobile shop.

Based in Blackpool, every week it works its way daily southwards across this particular area of the Welsh borders, kicking off in Shrewsbury and reaching our local emporium on the aforesaid day. The large, spotlessly white trailer lets down a side to make a counter, and three assistants cannot sell the fish fast enough.

That bravura one associates with market stalls abroad, with their keen sense of display, may be missing, but the heaps of haddock, mackerel, sardines, salmon, trout and cod gleam with a kind of effulgence. The kippers are cured at some Scottish loch and the smoked haddock is the real stuff, a variegated, muted ochre colour, a living riposte to that which is dyed saffron yellow.

A Friendship Recalled

FYNES MORYSON is one of my favourite early travellers to Italy. Taking a short break of a couple of days in Florence recently and visiting the Pitti Palace, I was reminded of that man's pride on seeing a portrait of 'Elizabeth our famous Queen'. Here she still is, refulgent in silver besprinkled with jewels and pearls, her legendary long fingers twitching a fan. Moryson saw this painting only a few years on from her defeat of the mighty Armada of Catholic Spain, to which the Florentine Grand Duke Ferdinand contributed. But, Fynes was told, she was there 'for the admiration of her vertues'.

Close to the Uffizi is a museum that people rarely visit, the Museo di Storia della Scienza. Here too is another outpost of Elizabethan England in the form of a showcase of instruments that were bequeathed to the Grand Dukes by the bastard son of Elizabeth's favourite, the Earl of Leicester. Not that Sir Robert Dudley ever accepted his illegitimacy. Handsome and brilliant, he is best remembered for leaving England with the beautiful daughter of Sir Robert Southwell in tow disguised as a page boy. But the showcase is full of mathematical and nautical instruments, one bearing the Queen's arms, testimony to a man who was a loss to maritime England. Reading him up, what struck me most was the perfectly enormous number of children he had – twenty in all, seven daughters by one wife, whom he repudiated, and thirteen more sons as well as daughters by Elizabeth Southwell.

Now, had he lived three centuries later he would have ended up in the English cemetery to which we also made a pilgrimage. Today this erupts out of a sea of traffic in an area that was then outside the walls of the city, an oval island held in by iron railings. Within, a craggy escarpment, rising a bit like a ship from a stormy sea, is thick with broken columns, crosses, headstones and busts of worthies. It has the appearance of having run out of space with people buried upright. Still, there it is, to misquote Rupert Brooke, another 'corner of a foreign field that is for ever England'.

WALKING TO WORK

∽

I WALK to work these days, or so my wife laughingly tells me. For I have a rule of life which cheers me immensely, that of walking round the garden immediately after breakfast, before going into my writing room. Off I go, togged for whatever weather, to make the same circuit from yew to kitchen garden, moving from east to west.

How fortunate I am to start my day noting, for example, that the crown imperials are at their height, or that the garlic we bought on the Quai des Fleurs in Paris is doing well. I contrast it in my mind with the decades spent sandwiched on the London Underground, gasping for air, and count my blessings.

DECLINE AND FALL?

∽∽∽

ON Easter Day, our church will be much fuller than usual, perhaps with as many as sixty communicants. A sense of joy will fill the air and everywhere there will be flowers and smiles. For those who come near the building only twice a year, it will provide a comforting sight. But the average weekly turnout is, in fact, fifteen or so. Most of these will not see fifty again, and many not sixty, and there are few signs of any young ones stepping forward to fill the gaps.

There are five churches in all in this benefice, and a forward projection on present evidence can only mean shedding three of these within the next twenty years. But no one wants to face that fact, or the greater one that the Church of England is still working within a medieval framework that cries out to be restructured. I am an optimist by nature, but that positive spirit needs to be fired by a vision which takes me forward beyond the year 2000. That perspective must be there, but I sense a reluctance by those who should lead, for the necessary changes would mean letting go of so much. This Easter I shall feel like one of Milton's hungry sheep who looks up and is not fed.

EASTER FLOWERS

෨෨

EASTER has come and gone, but the flowers in the church on Low Sunday, which follows Easter Day, remain. They are not quite the same, however, for they have been picked over for deadheads and replenished with new blooms to make good the gaps. It has not been easy this year, with everything at least a month in advance.

Every church has its flower-arranging rota, usually pinned up on the noticeboard. At Easter the flowers trespass out of the chancel along the nave windowsills and onto the font cover. The shop-bought arum lilies stick out a mile against the home-nurtured sprays of cherry and apple blossom, evergreen yew and laurel and cascades of narcissi. This is the loveliest of all seasons in a country church.

SHAKESPEARE'S 400TH BIRTHDAY

THE red cross of St George flutters from the flagpole of a nearby church on April the twenty-third, a reminder of our demoted national saint. At Stratford-upon-Avon, that day is still celebrated as being the traditional one of Shakespeare's birth. We know that he was christened on the twenty-sixth, so that the convenient association of national saint and national poet must always have been an attractive one.

The occasion is marked by a procession through the streets by the mayor and civic dignitaries, with representatives of the Royal Shakespeare Company and distinguished guests. Almost thirty years ago I walked in that procession.

23 April 1964 was the four hundredth anniversary of the playwright's birth, an event graced by a gargantuan exhibition in which I had responsibility for the Elizabethan portraits. Many were the woes that beset that spectacle, ending almost two years later in a welter of lawsuits and recriminations.

But let not those painful memories dim the glory of the great day, for it had a brilliance. Ambassadors of all the nations stood by flagpoles and, after a fanfare, unfurled their flags. Then a procession was formed to Holy Trinity Church. Everyone in it had to carry some kind of floral tribute, and I recall ordering one of herbs and flowers mentioned in the plays.

It arrived looking like a Victorian posy and I clutched it like a bridesmaid, bringing up the rear of the cavalcade neck and neck with the actress Leslie Caron, then married to the Royal Shakespeare Theatre's director, Peter Hall.

The rain tended to come and go, but despite a degree of chaos there was a sense of history. The great moment came as we entered the church to the sound of the organ. There, in a sanctuary to the left, was the bard's wall tomb, from which he presided with pen in hand, rather like an accountant totting up the bills. But beneath him spread a stunning sight, a mountain of spring flowers scenting the air, an effect made almost hallucinatory by the sunlight bestowing on them, through the stained-glass windows, pools of deepest ruby and amethyst.

Shortly afterwards, at the grand luncheon, I was brought sharply down to earth by a panic-stricken voice whispering in my ear, 'We've mislaid Shakespeare's will.'

SLIDING

I ALWAYS regard lecturing outside the metropolis as a hazard. It is not the audiences, which can be five or five hundred, but the mechanics of slide projection. One would never believe that one lived in the age of new technology, as projectors blow up, a spaghetti-junction of cable sprawls across the hall, lights fail and a far too small screen is balanced on anything to hand to enable the audience to see the image.

Not so this time, however. The Hereford Red Cross turned out to be a powerhouse of real organizational efficiency, transforming the Shire Hall into a working lecture theatre in no time, mastering the lighting switchboard and setting up trestle tables as wine bars to further boost the fund-raising.

Evenings like this go on in every part of the country, and have done so throughout this century. There is a kind of choreography attached to the organizers who converge on the place early and leave late. Whole families are dragooned into action, taking tickets, acting as ushers, laying out glasses, arranging chairs, selling wine or raffle tickets, operating the projector or dimming the lights. Then, suddenly, it is all over, dismantled and packed into the boots of cars, and the hall is left looking as though nothing had taken place.

TARRAGON

ᕔᕔᕔ

TARRAGON is a herb that I really miss in the winter months, and when the young bright green shoots suddenly thrust up into the light, they are watched with keen anticipation of the culinary delights to come. First, there will be enough to tuck two leaves at the bottom of *oeufs en gelée*, then a few more to be chopped and scattered into *oeufs à la crème*, or kneaded into seasoned butter and stuffed into the cavity of a trout. But all this is preliminary to the great moment of cooking one's first

tarragon chicken of the season. The new leaves seem
to have a freshness and a pungency of flavour which
is never the same later in the year, when the plant
rampages across the herb bed, and throws up spikes five
foot high with coarse, dull green leaves.

These days I prefer a more abstemious version of the
dish, avoiding a sea of cream. Instead, the chicken carcass
is filled with garlands of the herb wrapped round lemon
quarters, and roasted. A separate sauce of stock, tarragon
vinegar, lemon and the fresh herb is made. It is not
long before the intoxicating aroma spreads through the
kitchen and on up through the house, telling everyone
that it is spring and that the long months of savaging only
the bay and the rosemary have reached their end.

Soon there will be enough tarragon to harvest bunches
to make that most delicious of vinegars. We always hang
on to wide-mouthed glass jars so that we can fill them
with white-wine vinegar and spices, and then push in
whole stems of tarragon wrapped round in verdant

festoons. Few sights are more delectable than these bottles placed to catch the sunlight filtering through them from the kitchen windows, the beams catching the amber shades of the liquid, in which the leaves seem like fronds of seaweed wrenched from the ocean's floor.

JOGGING THE SIGHT

EVERY other day I go for a jog before lunch through the Herefordshire countryside, along loops of anything between four and eight miles in length. This began a decade ago, like so many things in middle age, in an effort to keep the body from falling apart. No other pursuit has matched it for making me so acutely conscious of the countryside and its seasons.

Hedgerows have become objects of absorbing interest as leaves come and go, fruits ripen and fall, or a frond of wild honeysuckle snakes its way upwards through branches of beech and crataegus. Often the banks below are dappled with bluebells and cowslips. Sometimes, I just have to stop and take in what Botticelli would have loved to have painted.

FIN DE SIÈCLE

EVERY period has its own ethos. As I look out on the flowers and fresh acid greens of spring, I am aware that they are at variance with the mood of the times. We gaze at nature's unending natural optimism which spells out hope each year in spring.

Thank heaven for that, for otherwise the mind seems overcast, as though one perceived the world through a black veil. I conjure up images of what seems to me to be the spirit of our era, one caught in earlier ages and familiar to any who tread the corridors of history. The 1590s was one such decade, with its striking contrast between the flower-strewn Golden Age – built by propagandists around the Virgin Queen – and the cruel realities of acute agricultural depression with failed harvests, a disastrous war in Ireland, and the restlessness of a new generation tired of an old lady at the helm. This was an age of 'sable-coloured melancholy'.

Or think of the close of the last century: on the one hand the brittle confidence of the upper classes as presented on stage by Oscar Wilde, on the other, the reality of their failure, as country house culture began to collapse and the long series of dissolutions got under way. In the countryside, as agriculture slumped, there was rural poverty on an appalling scale.

These reflections came into focus during a call to our local bank, in which a chance remark was made that the recession was now hitting Herefordshire. This is a remote county where the pendulum swings are rarely felt dramatically, but this time it is different. Any short walk or drive from this house tells the story. There are 'For Sale' signs everywhere, sometimes almost in rows, but nothing is selling.

The horror of chicken-broiler houses multiplies across the landscape – one means whereby farmers seek to avert ruin. Then there are the fields given over to cider apples and those earmarked for 'set-aside'. Everywhere bed-and-breakfast facilities are on offer. A local farmer's wife has even opened a day-nursery for tiny tots. And if we drive into Hereford or Ross-on-Wye the story is the same. Many shops stand empty. Most are in the grip of perpetual seasonal offers. And these are only the random impressions of the eye. What lies beneath the surface must be far worse.

But then I contrasted all that gloom with the joy of a visit to the Kilvert Gallery at Clyro, which exhibits and encourages young artists. There was an exhibition of the work of a young potter who specializes in making the most glorious, dotty ceramic food. My wife and I bought two pieces and felt a glow about seeing new talent coming to fruition.

CAT CAKE

∾⟡∾

WE have a friend who is even dottier about her animals than we are about our elephantine black cat, the Reverend Wenceslas Muff. Once, I remember, she gave a party, at the climax of which five Yorkshire terriers burst into the room like a cabaret chorus, each with a large, different-coloured bow tied on as a topknot. Now *en passant* she told us of one cat's nineteenth birthday, celebrated 'of course' by a party with a cake made of Whiskas, topped by candles and with a message on it. Such lunacy is as endearing as it is harmless, and it sharply reminded me of the day when our daily solemnly announced to my wife: 'I have given Sir Roy his coffee and Sir Muff his elevenses.'

TULIPOMANIA

꒰꒱

TULIP vases have always intrigued me. More than twenty years ago I purchased a modern Portuguese one in white porcelain, and placed tulip flowerheads in each of the nozzles – but the effect was not as fantastic as I had hoped.

Cecil Beaton had a small blue and white Delft one on a console table in his dining room at Reddish. It was a monument to ceramic restoration, for Cecil, like many others, believed that one filled the crock with earth and bulbs, and out of the nozzles the flowers would spring. Instead, one morning, he was confronted with a depressing heap of broken china and soil; it had exploded overnight.

Recently, however, I was forced to research the subject properly for a television sequence, using one of the five-foot-high Delft tulip vases in the Queen's Gallery at Hampton Court. These extravagant vases were made as a special line for the flower-struck Mary II.

Their correct designation is flower pyramids, and into them would be piled an explosion of seasonal blooms. We arrived on the day with bundles of yellow-and-red-striped parrot tulips, anemones in jewel shades, rusty orange crown imperials, luminous blue grape hyacinths, deep purple checked fritillaries, and auriculas like Genoese cut velvet.

It took me an hour to arrange them, but the result was stunning. I stood back in wonder. In its day, such an exotic display was real ostentation, for not only were the vases costly but so, too, were the flowers, in a period when tulip bulbs changed hands at legendary prices.

The Dutch at William III's restored palace of Het Loo have a charming tradition of filling all their historic Delftware flower vases once a year on Princess Juliana's birthday. What a lovely idea it would be to copy for our Queen's birthday, bringing momentary sparkle to Hampton Court's all-too-dead state rooms.

CHANCE ENCOUNTER

∾

WE stopped in Burford the other day, on our way home, for a quick pub lunch, but as we strolled from the car park a mass of plants for sale caught our eye. They were banked before the railings of a handsome late Victorian villa, with a wonderful small Victorian front garden, circular, its railinged bed still intact at the centre.

My eye then fell on dwarf trees, willows and prunus, grafted as tiny standards, and I was wondering who had had the imagination to do this when the owner appeared. He was dressed like an Edwardian head gardener, with a flat checked hat, a moustache of *belle époque* proportions, a green apron tied around him, and a tweed jacket over it.

I asked him about the front garden with its minute circular drive, when a path up the centre to the front door would have been so much more convenient. His grandmother, aged ninety-three, had told him that had been *de rigueur* in her day in order to make the garden seem larger and grander than it was.

There was nothing of the garden centre about this establishment. One left reflecting on the rarity of being able to talk to the person who had actually presided over every stage in the life of the plants we purchased.

A VISIT TO KING'S LYNN

KING'S LYNN has entered my life twice recently, and there have been few rediscoveries which have given me greater pleasure. I am sure that if I were a local I would know of terrible conservation and other battles, but the occasional visitor is struck by the genuine felicity with which the old town has been preserved as an entity of delight, but with no trace of mummification.

Early in the morning we were able to look down on the Tuesday market – where at six the stalls were going up fast, with their froth of produce and fabric – across to the extraordinary architecture of what turned out to be the Corn Exchange. When we first glimpsed it at a distance we thought it must have been a Catholic church put up soon after Emancipation in 1829, for it looked as if it had been lifted out of a piazza in Borromini's Rome. But no, it was secular mid-Victorian, and categorized neatly by Pevsner, which I looked up on our return, as 'jolly and vulgar'.

The walk from here along King Street to the Saturday

market must rank as one of the most pleasing of urban experiences. Inevitably, it has been tidied up and sanitized since the noise, bustle and squalor of the days when it was a working port. It was the simplicity and domesticity of it which struck me most. Even its grand statements – like the famous Custom House, with its statue of Charles II, which my wife had to draw as an art student – are carefully modulated. Slip alleys led down to the quayside lined with old Tudor buildings put to new use. The Elizabethan addition to the medieval Guildhall, although using the same honey-coloured stone and flint, was assertively of its own period, with its classical pilasters and Gloriana's arms blazed above its windows. Did the citizens of those days, I wondered, feel the shock of the new?

Parallel with King Street ran High Street, a busy pedestrianized mall with all those shops that ensure the good people of King's Lynn do not inhabit a stage set populated only with shops selling pot-pourri and craft potttery. On the whole they had got the balance right.

CAT MAGIC

∾❖∾

WHEN the nepeta in our garden froths in pale lilac profusion in high summer, it never ceases to astonish me. The reason is a simple one, for as soon as the growing year starts, its tiny new shoots are savaged by the Reverend Wenceslas Muff. The main planting is in a central bed in the rose garden around an old urn, and its purpose is to provide a summer display in succession to an array of tulips.

From the moment when a warm March day encourages the first grey-green leaves tentatively to emerge, I start discerning the large, furry form of Muff marching through the tulip sentinels, bent on demolishing any evidence of growth.

What is more surprising is that his access to fresh nepeta seems to make him extremely scornful of the dried stuff. This usually takes the form of a cloth mouse stuffed with catmint. My supply of these comes from Culpeper in Covent Garden, although Harrods also has a lively line. There on the counter was the basket, piled high not only with mice but also with catnip fish. No point in the latter, I told the assistant. Dangling the object above the cat by its string tail is half the fun.

The attitude of Muff's city cousins, however, is quite different. Recently, I took two catnip mice to a pair of gardenless, flat-dwelling cats and had the pleasure of staring at the effect on these creatures for twenty minutes or so. They jumped in the air, rolled over and even sat up on their haunches, hugging the mice in a frenzy of grateful acrobatics. One turned upside-down and just stared at me for most of the evening in gratitude.

Armed with this success I arrived home to find Muff sitting in a heap by the Aga, looking bored. Remedy to hand, or so I thought, I dangled a new catnip mouse beneath his nose in keen anticipation of the delight to follow.

Not a murmur. Just the pat of a paw brushing the

object to one side in disgust, and a disdainful glance at me, after which he composed himself into sphinx-like hauteur.

HOUSE MARTINS

∽∾∽

JUST why I should have an affection for our house martins, I have never quite known or, to be honest, perhaps I do. We moved in on 3 May 1973, the day that they returned for the summer to the house. They struck a much needed romantic omen of good fortune, doubly welcome after we had been greeted with the news that our furniture van had crashed outside Gloucester. We had to spend the rest of the day presiding over the delivery of what looked like pieces of firewood and pottery remains.

Our great source of information as to the house martins' annual imminence is our local garage owner. The car was getting its usual top-up and check-up after church on a Sunday in mid April, when we were told that the first martins had been sighted. One usually spots one of these emissaries as it swoops and circles the house, inspecting the condition of what is left of last year's detached and semi-detached residences.

From the first week of May, the martins furiously repair and build their nests. The only drawback to them is that we will be stuck with the disagreeable task of hacking off their droppings from the glass roof of part of our kitchen, after their departure for sunny climes.

COLUMBINE WITHOUT
HARLEQUIN

∞∽∾∾

I WAS first really entranced by the beauty of aquilegias in Aspen, Colorado, in the middle of the 1980s. We were at a conference there, raising the flag for British design, but breakfast each morning found us on sunny terraces looking across swathes of aquilegias growing wild on the hillside. Up until then I had been aware only of the self-seeded kind which invariably popped up where we did not want them and were almost without exception a funereal purple.

But, oh, what lovely flowers they are. My wife began to grow them alongside the vegetables in the kitchen garden, and initially I showed reluctance to transplant the proffered young ones to the 'state apartments'.

How wrong I was. The variety called 'McKana's Giant Mixed' has given enormous pleasure, with its feathery, grey-green leaves and incredibly complicated blooms, in a new flower garden outside the breakfast room window.

From there we can see them nodding, intricate confections in shades of pink, yellow, crimson, purple and white, any of which, enlarged, would be a milliner's triumph for Ascot. And yet, like pinks, there is an old-fashioned quality to them which is beguiling. They do not shout for attention. The eye must learn to settle and drink in the subtlety of the convolution of their petals and the extraordinarily glorious orchestration of colour that they present.

Chiltern Seeds list more than twenty varieties, which just goes to show how far we have yet to voyage in our cultivation of the columbine.

Even more delicate than our own feelings are those of the Reverend Wenceslas Muff. The time-honoured ritual each morning of stretching his forepaws and asking to be admitted to the drawing room has had to cease. The room is now empty and the windowsill on which he sat, his huge tail twitching in response to his observation, is no more. Although I tell him of the delights to come, it fails to cut much ice, and he has reordered his day. Back upstairs he goes to a little warm rug in our dressing room where he hugs one of his two catnip mice, Tesco or Culpeper, whose names tell all as to their origin, and falls asleep, only to spring to life late in the afternoon when the workmen have left.

Animals have an innate good sense. We only wish that we could rearrange our day in emulation of his.

HONEYSUCKLE FOR REMEMBRANCE

THE honeysuckle in the hedgerows was particularly good this year, with huge flowerheads in shades of white, cream and ochre running through to pink. No amount of mechanical hedge laceration seemed to have impeded their vigour as they thrust themselves through a tangle of quickthorn. In the garden, four standard *Lonicera periclymenum* 'Serotina', which I bought in the garden centre at Cranborne Manor, also looked better than ever. Trained over domes of blue-painted wire, the flowers were a jostling profusion of vinous deep pink, whose luminosity was akin to that of stained glass.

But the honeysuckle we treasure most has quite

another story. It goes back almost twenty years to my mother-in-law's last illness, when an old schoolfriend brought a bunch of wild and garden flowers for her bedside. They came from the garden of the Old Rectory at Wootton, near Oxford, an early work of Capability Brown which was later enriched by the green fingers of an Edwardian clergyman called Frank Marriott, who transformed it into a plant treasury. From my one visit to the house I remember the huge glazed frames which covered the tender plants on the verandah in winter.

After my mother-in-law's death, my wife took the sprigs of honeysuckle from the bunch of flowers, and planted them. Surprisingly, some took root, and one in particular throve and was eventually ready to be moved. We planted it where it would scramble over a wooden pergola arch leading to a small orchard. Few plants have suffered so much – from being liberally soaked with weedkiller by a well-meaning gardener to enduring twenty-four degrees of frost. But it survived. Three years ago it had to be moved again, and now it romps away, a froth of indescribable gold over a trellis tunnel in the kitchen garden.

So much memory is entwined in that one plant, taking us back to sunshine days before 1914, to two young girls playing in a rectory garden, not knowing what fate had in store for them. Strange to think that, when we are no more, it will be just another honeysuckle.

Keeping Them Guessing

BEFORE the new season's produce starts coming, there is the usual excavation of the deep freezes to see what can be devised from the remnants of last year. Gooseberries, for instance, silently reproach me, as the fresh ones are within an ace of harvesting for the summer's first creamy fool or pie. The autumn fruits offer no such reproach as yet, and their juices, stored in discarded plastic water bottles, have proved a rich quarry of ideas for the table.

Medlar, blackberry and quince now provide the base for delicious ice creams and sorbets.

Of these, it is the quince which has prompted what I consider to be my latest culinary *chef d'oeuvre*. For a lunch party, scoops of quince ice cream are placed on turn-of-the-century Venetian dishes, its intriguing pink-orange colour set off to advantage against the emerald, gold-spangled stripes of the glass. Two delicate biscuits are arranged to one side, and a scattering of toasted almonds or a dribble of quince syrup complete the picture. Each dish is then set on a porcelain plate and thence to the table. A certain puzzled silence always follows the first mouthful. 'What is it?' 'Guess,' I reply. People rarely do.

SUMMER LOSS

ANY summer of Mediterranean heat means that that staff of life, the Aga, is turned off. The kitchen, as a result, is inevitably cooler, but it is as though some large domestic animal had ceased to radiate its loved presence to its owners. The whole orientation of kitchen life completely changes, as well as what can and cannot be done. The cat alone still sits in front of it, oblivious that the *raison d'être* for his presence there has gone.

We, on the other hand, are more than keenly aware of our loss. Anything to do with yeast suddenly comes to a halt. My wife's minor wine factory goes into abeyance, and the manufacture of home-baked bread ceases as we live off the hump of winter buried in the deep freeze.

Glass bottles and jars can no longer be dried off on the Aga's back shelf, or tea towels on the rack in front. And food and plates can no more be kept deliciously warm in the lower oven.

It is curious how the Calor gas stove never assumes the status of that enamelled gentle giant, which takes up a huge amount of space and seems to hold the whole house in its embrace. I look out at the straw-like grass and secretly long for the day of its rekindling.

'THE MOLE LADY'

∾

THE moles are back. Across the greensward of the Silver Jubilee Garden the turf is broken and little heaps begin to appear. A perfect garden picture is desecrated at its apogee.

Our molecatcher proved rather elusive. I got on to her by ringing up the local town hall and asking for pest control. The fact that she lived in Rose Cottage sounded suitably rural and she arrived, white-haired and pink-cheeked, attired in the guise of a *cavaliero* by Callot in tweed kneebreeches. She had learned the craft from an old molecatcher skilled in mixing the deadly potions, and in the habits of these black gentlemen.

Traps were set, marked by twigs, and I was given cheerful homilies on the ways of moles which, in one part of the garden, had established a veritable Clapham Junction. She used to return a few weeks later with a bag for the corpses, once as many as nine. These had to be despatched post haste for skinning and a fate, I suppose, as someone's cosy collar. She always referred to our garden as her 'Versailles garden'.

We thought we had got rid of most of the moles and two winters ago our part-time gardener, Wilf, skimmed back the turf in the formal gardens and filled in the corridors. It was an extraordinary sight to see the garden criss-crossed with a myriad of tunnels. And now they are back again.

THE GHOSTS OF VERSAILLES

MISS MOBERLY and Miss Jourdain's famous 'adventure' first cast its spell over me as a schoolboy, in the post-war period when it had not been debunked. The idea of two people losing themselves in the grounds of the Petit Trianon one August day in 1901, and stepping back suddenly two centuries in time was the most compulsive of ghost stories. Their book described how they had encountered court officials in tricorn hats holding staves, and seen a garden kiosk long since vanished, as indeed had the little bridge they crossed.

'Everything suddenly looked unnatural, therefore unpleasant; even the trees behind the building seemed to have become flat and lifeless . . . There were no effects of light and shade and no wind stirred in the trees. It was all intensely still.' And on they went, to be overcome with horror by a pockmarked man in a black cloak, a messenger who appeared and warned them not to pass that way, and, nearer to the Petit Trianon, Marie

Antoinette sketching. When I first visited Versailles, I longed for such an experience.

The fact that that book went through five editions between 1901 and 1955 is some testimony to the fascination of more than one generation. This all came to mind when I read the book by Lucille Iremonger, *The Ghosts of Versailles*, which in 1955 effectively demolished the story.

It is a brilliant, brittle study, out of which the two maiden Oxford ladies emerge rather badly, as they seem to have embroidered somewhat – but one was not to know that at the time, when such a story seemed to encapsulate a proximity to the past only a trifle more heightened than that undergone in so many historical sites.

Now one can see it in a line of descent through the historical novel and the history painting, down through the historical play and film to the *son et lumière* and waxwork displays of our own time. But I am still left with more than a slight hankering after 'an adventure'.

CAT AMBULANCE

THE Reverend Wenceslas Muff has had tonsillitis. One misses speech even more when an animal is ill than when it cannot tell you which tin of food it would like. When at last we twigged that our black cat was off-colour we were faced with whisking him to the vet, an operation involving stealth akin to a high-security exercise. The car was covertly moved to hand, and his carrying basket placed near but hidden. Suddenly my wife seized him, put him quickly into the basket, and I fastened the containing metal grill. He did not like it.

Julia drove and I placed the basket on my lap with Muff facing me. I talked to him all the time but it was no use: he started to cry, and then we both felt harrowed. Mercifully, it was only a short distance, and once on the vet's table Muff behaved impeccably. Vague feelings akin to parental pride took over as he stood erect to be examined and purred while being injected. We were given pills for him.

Making a cat swallow a pill is another of those operations which have to be crept up on. By a series of coded gestures my wife and I would swing into action. Julia picked him up and held him upside down, securing his paws, while I forced open his mouth and popped the pill in. After a couple of goes I became quite proficient, acquiring the trick of slightly shaking his head to ensure the pill went down.

Fax of Life

∽∾∾∽

THE Garden Room is a misnomer, for it houses the deep-freezes and many things that keep a house going, like bubble plastic and old cartons neatly stacked in order. Its real focus these days are the implements of the new technology, the photocopier and the fax machine. That we have one of the latter at all is a monument to the failure of the postal system in rural areas, for it can take a week for a letter to reach London first class from the Welsh Borders.

British Telecom, unlike the Post Office, was a monument to alacrity of service, as indeed were our local office suppliers who also supply young men used to instructing people like myself, whose encounter with a fax machine was akin to that of a first glimpse of the Rosetta stone. Now it is up and working we wonder how we ever managed before, and speculate as to how it would have changed the lives of our literary predecessors.

PRINNY'S ARCADIA

∞∞∞

WE were lucky on the day that we went to Virginia Water. The sun shone, the lake shimmered, and the encompassing banks were verdant and still quite fresh in their greens. All landscape is a palimpsest and just as complicated to disentangle in terms of its layers as any church or country house. This time I was in search of George IV, for it was here that the bewigged and plump monarch would wend his way seeking pleasure. By then he feared the gaze of the outside world and so the Great Park was sealed off, and he and his cronies made their way to the waters by means of hidden winding paths.

The sheer size of the lake astonished me. It was the largest made in Georgian England by that unpleasant character, 'Butcher' Cumberland. His cascade is still there, splendid but for a road winding too close to it. But where is Prinny? The famous Chinoiserie fishing temple has long since gone, although one can etch it on the lakeside in one's imagination as Windsor Great Park's riposte to Brighton Pavilion. The boat house and the Chinese Island, too, have gone, as have, inevitably, the exotic tents and pavilions that stood close to the water's edge, although our guide talked of lighting upon what may have been their foundations.

Soaring above the trees we glimpsed the tower of the miniature Gothick Fort Belvedere, now remembered more for Mrs Simpson than as a site for George IV to celebrate his birthday. But the extraordinary ruins of Leptis Magna – the Temple of Augustus as they were called – still stand, or at least in part. Here, beneath the public road, was one of the King's hidden ways which had been disguised as a triumphal arch. This had once been flanked on the lakeside with a sweep of marble columns in perspective, so that the King would have erupted through the arch like a Roman emperor in triumph.

How wonderful that at least this part of one of Regency landscape gardening's greatest set pieces survives to evoke something of its former glory.

TUSCANY

୧୬ଡ଼ୄ

EVERYONE else was upstairs, or rather up the flight of steps which led up to the loggia to the villa, drinking coffee and sampling Tuscan fare at what I suppose was a kind of brunch. I had taken myself away, stolen down the steps and sat on a warm stone bench that was embedded in the wall embowered with jasmine, and looked onto the landscape. The view was stupendous, for the villa, built early in the sixteenth century, began its life as a hunting lodge perched high on one of the hills that encircle Lucca. An arc of the purest blue held in a panorama with which I first fell in love in 1955: that of Tuscany.

In the distance to the left I could see Lucca with its renaissance fortifications mantling it firmly in; to the right, Pisa with that curious tower which forever leans and never falls and which can, on a very clear day, just be seen; while dimly beyond, there was the port of Livorno and the sea. Even now each of the towns looks like one of those buildings donors hold in their hands and proffer to God.

Despite the proliferation of buildings, the effect from afar remained that of landscape. One was aware of its layers receding through an endless permutation of greens: yellow into grey into blue and purple, with the strong dark verticals of cypress trees punctuating it. In the foreground stretched an attempt at an English flower border, with spikes of pale violet and amber irises and a terrace wall which together formed the staffage. Sometimes the sun would hit a moving vehicle, but most of the time it all seemed empty, motionless and extraordinarily beautiful.

CHICKEN OUT

✤

IF I was asked to name one of the few things that have really blighted our joy in country life over the past two decades, it would have to be the battery chicken industry. Some years ago, when the fate of these creatures started to seep into the public arena, we began to avoid eating them, our minds conditioned not only by the horror stories in the media but by local experiences of what can happen when a shed catches fire or is blown over into the next field.

Although the Herefordshire landscape is blotted by them, we do not, as yet, actually look out on one. Our curse is the smell. This filthy and, at times, suffocating stench blows over from the nearest encampment some three fields away. A garden is not only a visual and aural experience. It is also one of smell, whether responding to the intoxicating sweetness of honeysuckle or the elegant scent of an old rose. That pleasure can now be obliterated for days on end as we are forced to inhale the polluted air.

The country has always been a place for smells, some of them pretty pungent. But factory-farming methods now seem to be polluting the air in a manner reminiscent of that engendered in towns by factories during the Industrial Revolution of the previous century.

LORD OF THE DANCE

∽�∾

I THOUGHT that my dancing days had long since gone, until I found myself at a conference dinner in a hotel on Loch Lomond. The thought of what was billed as a Scottish evening, with bagpipes, haggis and the rest of it, made me shudder. But I was wrong. I had forgotten the magic ability of those old community dances to get everyone, young and old, onto the floor. The leader of the three-piece band took us through our paces with each dance, and then we were off.

Hands alternately linked and parted, partners twirled, lost and gained. Circling and reversing, advancing and retreating, human arches formed to pass under in procession or to act as gateways to those beyond. The hours fled by in what was a timeless scene which, but for our clothes, could have been any period during the last century or more. All one was conscious of was the rhythm of the dancers, laughter and eyes bright with happiness. Could any memory be more precious or more beautiful?

GOLD IN THE GARDEN

∽�∾

COLOUR in your garden – how often have I heard that phrase and thought, inevitably, of Penelope Hobhouse's marvellous book? But, increasingly, we find ourselves experimenting with colour in another way, painted onto the hard artefacts which contribute to any garden's composition. We have for that the sanction of history, for the great gardens of the past were a riot of painted effects.

Avenues of trees could be terminated with a triumphal arch in *trompe l'oeil* painted on canvas. That I would find difficult to take. The pagoda at Kew had roofs of shimmering golden tiles and no fewer than eighty golden dragons as gable finials. That is a sight I would have responded to, glistening and flashing in the summer sun.

But today's small gardens call perhaps for a more cautious approach. We started by painting seats, trellis and wire dome supports a variety of ship blue. As it weathers it forms a perfect foil for foliage and flower, avoiding the strident contrast of the all-prevailing white. Blue wire obelisks to support roses were given golden finials, and that became a turning point. Gold in the garden has since become an obsession.

The bill for the gilded finials has, however, prompted a search for a passable substitute. In this quest we have been aided by our local painter, always game for any of our eccentricities. With him we have run through a whole gamut of commercial golds on the antlers of a recumbent stag.

For months the result was never anything but a sludgy, shiny brown. But perseverance brings its rewards, and he arrived one day with what has turned out to be an acceptable substitute. Layers of it were applied to a stone ball which now sits on top of a column at the close of a vista, catching the sunlight in a way which can be described as convincing. Fortuntely, that is sited well away from those gold-leafed finials, for every time I spy them, doubts begin to assail my mind. But surely gold in the gardens of the past cannot have always been twenty carat?

PENGUIN MONARCHS

∽∽

RESHELVING books after redecoration. What a jog to the memory that can be. About fifteen years ago we decided to try and collect all the King Penguin series, and we now have nearly all of them. Both of us are indebted to these books for opening doors to the imagination in the post-war years. As I put them on the shelf I turned the pages of the one on misericords and found that it was a gift to me from a friend in 1958. He died young, after years of struggling with an appalling illness, but he was the first person to teach me how to look at the inside of a church. Perched on the back of his motorbike, we hurtled around the countryside on what we called church crawls.

Very High Church we were at the time, and I remember Cedric, in an aesthetic rage, removing all the brass pots from a dingy altar. He told me that clerics who wished to be rid of these abominations would wait until the weather was really cold, fill them with water overnight, and return to find them exploded into pieces in the morning.

British Military Uniform was another present, this time in 1946, when I was fourteen but already in love with the history of dress. It introduced me to the work of James Laver, whom I later met, and remember as a superbly elegant speaker and raconteur. John Piper's

Romney Marsh we got the painter to sign. I recall trying to imitate his drawing technique when I was in the sixth form in 1952. I still have some of those early efforts, embodying a direction in life I might have taken, and certainly hankered for more than the museum cloister. But it was not to be.

DIGGING IT UP

ONE cloudless day we drove north into Shropshire for lunch with friends at Wenlock Abbey. Not far from the magic escarpment of Wenlock Edge nestles the delightful town of Much Wenlock, in the middle of which the abbey ruins and great house stand divided neatly, as it were, into public and private domains. The house was once the prior's lodgings, a handsome L-shaped range, holding within its arms a sundial, a broad expanse of verdant turf and an abundance of multi-coloured roses. In such a way the violence of a Tudor revolution, overlaid by the softening hand of Time, foliage and flower, now presents a tableau that seems both immutable and immemorial.

Although the abbey's roots stretch back as far as the seventh century, when it was founded by St Milburga, what we see today stems from its refounding in about 1080 as a Cluniac priory. I came across it several years ago when, as director of the Victoria & Albert Museum, I purchased a stunning and rare Romanesque lectern which had been excavated from the ruins. I felt rather guilty at having been instrumental in this piece leaving its historic home nine centuries after its creation. Our host pointed out where it used to stand in the prior's chapel, and his hospitality, I am glad to say, remained undiminished.

But the great excitement was to see the exacavations being undertaken in the chapel, now three feet below its normal floor level, and hear of the plethora of fragments that had been unearthed, which shed new light on the history of this quite extraordinary complex. We stood examining the convex holes which were sites on which lead had been melted before being worked into the abbey roof. The enthusiastic young archaeologist proffered me a dollop of medieval dung, explaining that the addition of some moisture would restore its malodorous quality. 'There's none of your poncy art history here,' he said. Nor indeed was there.

Suffolk Progress

THE Garden Trust movement is one of the exhilarating new impulses in what tends to be a doom-laden time. Its aim is to preserve our heritage of gardens and guard against their devastation through neglect or bad planning. It was in the interests of that cause that we wended our way to East Anglia where, hopefully, my lecture might raise a little cash for the Norfolk one. It is always a shot in the dark when one says 'Yes' to one of these invitations. The amazing fact is that, in nine cases out of ten, it means new friends and a host of happy, memorable experiences. And so it turned out to be.

In this mini, three-day progress I was struck in the houses and gardens which we visited by how each generation adapted to new circumstances, creating life-styles ensuring the vigour of country life into the new century. The young Bacons (theirs is the country's oldest baronetcy) at Raveningham, for instance, took the garden forward in time by siting handsome pieces by the sculptor of the house, Susan Bacon.

We also stopped to marvel at the results of Lady Tollemache's *furor hortensis* at Helmingham, sharing the excitement of the new greenhouse, the planting of a new parterre and, best of all, her own new garden, with the family armorial fret incorporated into its knots, now reaching maturity after a decade.

And then there were the Cargills, our hosts at Elsing Hall, a testament to reviving the fortunes of a house and finding a style which was a vigorous marriage of new and old. Modern works acquired from Angela Flowers looked stunning against the old walls, and bold sculptures in steel and terracotta arose amid the tangled romantic gardens. All these were signs of optimism, I thought, a signal perhaps that the country house could cease to be an icon of nostalgia and could once again resume its old role as a beacon of all that is new.

Return of the Hunter

∾⌦∾

A DISTANT, rather distorted trill is heard. The time is usually between five and six o'clock in the morning. My head is still lying on the pillow with eyes firmly shut when my ears take in this trumpet from afar. It is, of course, the Reverend Wenceslas Muff at the bottom of the stairs, with some victim trapped between his teeth. We lie in bed awaiting the presentation of the trophies of the chase. Next there is a sudden scuttle and he is up the stairs, still emitting purring trills. Is whatever it is alive or dead, we wonder? We pray for the latter as we tug our eyelids slowly apart, ready for the ensuing ritual.

Trot, trot, round the bed he goes. Muff being a chap, it is Julia who is the recipient of his game bag. He drops it by her and she anxiously peers down, stifling any natural reaction of having a blood-stained corpse dumped on the bedroom carpet, in favour of telling the murderer how wonderful he is. At least this time he has not jumped onto the bed with a live rabbit.

A mouse presents few problems for, once dead, there is little beyond a ballet around the bed while he leaps up and down tossing it in the air. Suddenly we hear a crunching sound which means that he has begun to consume his victim.

In the case of a rabbit the ritual is far more prolonged. Usually, the corpse is carried around for a large portion of the day, and laid in exhibition at strategic points until it, too, is devoured. Books on cat behaviour tell us it is their way of making up for our own inability to hunt.

Edible Still Life

∽∽

A REALLY hot summer is an excuse for alfresco lunch parties. Tables and chairs of all sorts are scattered across the grass and paving of a garden. Guests dress in a bewildering ragbag of clothes, with almost gypsy-like splashes of primary colour. And, due to the abundance of sun, hats of all sorts are worn, from ones in shapeless canvas to stylish panamas.

But the real glory is the food. Not just the choice of menu or the excellence of its taste, but the sense of presentation and spectacle. The accolade for this so far goes to a tableau of puddings cooked and staged, for that is the only word, by a designer friend of ours. Every course was beautiful, but this one had the advantage of being the last to be eaten so that it was able to take the

form of a still life in a room of its own. Along one side stretched a table with no fewer than twelve puddings displayed.

Ones such as a summer pudding on a glass cakestand or a triple-decker mounded up with meringues ranked as simple fare and mere foils to the main *tours de forces*. There was a chocolate pudding like a cabbage, darkly rich brown at its heart, and enfolded with huge chocolate leaves. A bowl, filled with nut-encrusted brandy snaps and pastel pink meringues, was scattered with crystallized primroses, while nearby a *bavarois* had been lined with slices of the tiniest swiss roll, giving it an all-over whirling pattern.

For a brief hour or two these masterpieces stood in all their glory as we ate the ham marbled with green herbs and the salmon encased in glazed scales of cucumber. But then sentence of execution was passed, and the massacre by spoon swiftly followed.

Parterre Perfect

☙

Few things have given me more pleasure than being asked to declare open the restored 1830 parterre flower garden at Audley End, in Essex. The opening was on a perfect summer's day when everything about the house, the garden, the park and the event itself represented English Heritage at its very best. As I had not been there since the 1960s, I was struck by the enormous improvements in presenting it to the public as a romantic, antiquarian compilation of the early nineteenth century, somewhat akin, I would suppose, to Charlecote: early Victorian Jacobean, but of a cosy kind, with wall-to-wall carpeting which would have astonished James I.

But, of all the delights, the parterre was the thing, a gigantic affair, a huge geometric pattern of flowerbeds on either side of a fountain stretching the whole width of the back of the house. When planted, it was the height of fashion, a pure expression of a period which revelled in embroidering phoney antiquity onto existing ancient manor houses. The parterre had survived in its original form until after the Second World War, but was then gradually eliminated, and almost ten years of archival and archaeological research were needed to recreate it.

The result is something quite glorious, not only to look down upon from above, but to stroll through. I was struck by the composition in which informality in the outer beds – a froth of china roses and perennials – contrasts with bedding-out at the centre. Thirty years on, the latter was to form the High Victorian style. But Audley End represents an intermediate stage – one that I found pleasing, and that caused me to rethink the long fashionable disdain for bedding-out.

THERE IS A TIDE . . .

❦

IT MADE me smile to read that the Historic Houses Association's report, *The Disintegration of the Country House*, was 'a deliberately polemical piece, clearly modelled on the seminal *Destruction of the Country House*'. In 1974, I was appointed director of the Victoria &

Albert Museum, and soon after, John Harris, the architectural historian, mooted the idea of an exhibition on the problems facing country houses, following a report by another old friend, John Cornforth.

One of the main reasons for wanting the V & A job was that I sensed a profound crisis in the national heritage, and thought that the museum would be an excellent vehicle for taking the message to a wider public. It was, however, politically tricky, for the museum was part of government and I was unable to utter one word which might cross official policy. The real worry was the wealth tax which was part of the opposition Socialist Party's agenda. When I became director, there was a Tory government, but by the time the exhibition opened, Labour was in power. I remember placing an embargo prohibiting the press from the opening party. I feared that it would ill serve the cause to have pictures of champagne-swilling country house owners in the papers.

Looking back, it required some bravery to mount that exhibition in a state-funded institution, using government money. But indeed the same team, which included Marcus Binney, went on in the 1970s to tackle churches and gardens. We had planned one on towns, but by then Lady Thatcher had come in and things took a very different direction. Which brings me back to where I began – that smile.

It crossed my face because in all things there are times and tides, and one of the important things in life is to spot them. Since 1974, the country house crisis has had an incredible run, but the 1990s are different. This decade is less about holding on to our past than about letting go in order to have a future. The country house lobby is beating a drum that sounds hollow. A new message is needed, which will square with the more forward-looking meritocratic society of the next century. However, the days of saying such things through museum polemic are long gone.

Out, Out Damned Spot . . .

◦⌒⌒◦

AUGUST is the tail end of the soft-fruit season. Nothing freezes better than raspberries, and black and red currants, so off we go, buckets in hand to the local selfpick, arrayed like peasants in *Eugene Onegin*. The buckets began their life with paste for wallpaper in them many years ago.

There is a deadly monotony about picking soft fruit, and one's hands are left stained as though one had committed one of the more ghastly mutilations in *Titus Andronicus*. The object of this exercise is the mass-production of summer puddings. Plastic containers which once held ice cream are now pressed into service as factory-line production is set into motion across the kitchen.

I pretend not to notice the horrendous ready-sliced loaf that I cut up and use to line the cartons, thinking how to mask the truth from any guest who consumes one. Sweat pours off me until I stand looking at the thirty or so puddings, all neatly sealed and ready to stack in the freezer. We never mind them out of season, and in consumption the drudgery of the making quite vanishes from the mind as one contemplates instead the luscious bitter sweetness of summer fruits.

COUNTESS MANQUÉ

∾⋈∾

MY wife had been working at Glyndebourne, so there had been a fair amount of commuting across country from Herefordshire to Sussex: not the most direct of routes, and a five-and-a-half-hour haul. One day we lightened our journey by turning off the road to look at Bisham church, near Henley, to see what always touches me as one of the great mortuary ensembles from the Elizabethan age: the tombs of the Hobys, including that man who was known as Mr Posthumous Hoby because his father died while his mother was still carrying him.

Here if anywhere are monuments to lost hopes and aspirations. Two marble knights lie side by side, their feet on the Hoby cognizance, the hawk; against a window arises a grey obelisk sprouting upwards from the outspread wings of four swans; but I stood overawed, above all, by the great tomb of that formidable old lady, Elizabeth Coke, Lady Hoby and later Lady Russell. Shrouded in the coffered veils of an aristocratic widow, she still dominates her dead. The light filtering into this chapel is a dappled one, caused by the Jacobean mullioned window and also by the refraction of the water of the nearby Thames, which runs within yards of the chancel.

Costard, in *Love's Labour's Lost*, when suddenly

confronted with a brilliant company, asked 'Which is the head lady?' and there is never a doubt here as we study the pale, stern face of her ladyship, wearing a countess's coronet to which she had no right, for her second, Russell, husband died before inheriting the title. She kneels facing the daughter who did achieve that distinction, Anne, who became Countess of Worcester. One of the joys of reading and writing history is to have friends in the past, for Anne and her sister Elizabeth, who kneels behind her mother, first crossed my path in John Nichols's *Progresses of Queen Elizabeth* thirty years before.

I left, moved by the confidence with which that age projected itself to posterity, and mused on how historic buildings legislation, the conservation lobby and practically every other protest group would ensure that no such ego trip would ever be allowed to occur again.

CUTTING A FIGURE

∾

I CAN never understand why people dislike hedge-cutting. August to me means above all the joy of cutting hedges, seemingly mile after mile of them, for we have cheerfully planted several furlongs, and continue to plant: hedges of yew, beech, laurel and − yes, I can anticipate the superior shudders − *Cupressus leylandii*. I am certain that, had they existed in the seventeenth century, they would have been planted everywhere.

The first summer we had our Herefordshire house I

crenellated the old thuya hedge up the drive. It gave me an enormous sense of achievement, for it turned a very dull piece of garden screening into something of delight, and above all, having altered it, I felt for the first time that the hedge really belonged to us. It was only recently that Rosemary Verey suddenly asked why I had not done the same thing to the field hedge on the opposite side. And so it was cut into swags and once more there came a sense of creation and possession.

In these balmy weeks it is out with the steps, the shears, the secateurs, the radio and my straw hat. I have never obeyed the rules. There is no batter on the yew hedges. I have never cut templates, preferring to do things by eye, fiddling with loops of string for cutting swags, and measuring distance by canes, and height by my own shoulders. There is no fancy framing for the topiary, which has been achieved simply by tying branches together with bits of string and snipping away. I am sure that I would have been fired by Le Nôtre or London and Wise, but no matter: my ambition to be the poor man's Henry Moore of topiary remains, after fifteen years, deeply fulfilling.

EDWARDIAN SUNSET

ഇൻകൗ

I HAD forgotten how beautiful the Scottish Lowlands were. On a recent tour I shephereded some twenty people around homes and gardens, at their peak a month later than those in the south, with roses in perfection. Never before have I so forcefully been struck by the confidence of the landed classes, in the years immediately before 1914, that their way of life was unassailable.

Out of the handful of houses we visited, no fewer than three had embarked on massive gardening schemes in the decade before the First World War. At Manderston, near Duns, Duveen supplied spectacular garden ornaments for the terracing near the house, and for the formal gardens which lay beyond gilded gates.

At Mellerstain, near Gordon, in 1909, Sir Reginald Blomfield started the re-landscaping of the terrain at the back of the house into Italianate terraces and flights of steps. These still hold house, garden, park and lake together in one stunning composition, even if one has to admit that its style is grander than the rear of Adam's somewhat nondescript castle. Both these schemes incorporated elaborate parterres which betokened an army of gardeners.

At Stobo Castle, near Peebles, the cricketer Hylton Philipson created a magical garden in the Japanese style (1909 to 1912). It wends its way through a valley beneath two artificial lakes, the source for the cascades and rushing water which animate the exotic planting of rare acers and flowering shrubs. This garden must be unique in Scotland, but I was sad to hear that its future may be under threat, due to problems with the water in the upper lakes.

Manderston and Mellerstain, however, are as glorious as on the day they were finished – monuments to survival and rationalization in terms of mechanization and the labour force. But what financial resources, what optimism and confidence these projects embodied at the time. I was left to ponder how many works of art would never have existed if their initiators could have known what was just around the corner.

SOME LIKE IT HOT

∾

THE grass beneath my writing room has slowly turned to a sickly straw colour. The heat has been relentless, day in and day out. Inside, the house takes on the atmosphere of glazed languor so brilliantly caught in the Visconti film, *The Leopard*. The lawn blinds remain firmly lowered, and the curtains are drawn in succession as the sun crosses the windows of the house.

Within, we move through a mysterious dappled shade, never quite total. The odd shaft of light, bleaching the colour out of the atmosphere, always penetrates somehow, and there are strange hazy patterns of light and dark suffused through layers of glazing bars, grills and shielding textiles.

Every so often, a little breeze momentarily lifts the papers on my desk, but it quickly subsides and they fall back again, seemingly exhausted by the heat, as though they had a life like our own.

Now is not the time to explore the loft, as I did one year, and found the temperature there soaring into the nineties. As it is, the heat rises in the house, and the bedrooms become havens of engulfing, balmy humidity. The air seems never to move, and at night one lies either on top of the bedclothes or covered only by a sheet, overcome with claustrophobia even though the window is flung wide to the night sky.

British houses were never built to accommodate the demands of a Mediterranean summer. There are no commodious, slatted outside shutters to reach out and close, no high ceilings for the circulation of the air, no marble or tiled floors for coolness.

Our architecture faces outward to the world, and there are no inward-looking, shady courtyards with trees and a trickling fountain to contemplate. Vainly I push my pen across the paper during the hours in which southern Europe sensibly enjoys its siesta.

TRAVELLING HATS

USUALLY, any venture into the garden signals rifling through the pile of old coats, scarfs, jackets, woollen hats, wellingtons and cloggies in the back hall. But in a hot summer our straw hats, normally relegated to a shelf in a back passage, are placed ready to hand. Straw hats are robust objects, made to last a lifetime, and fit to be passed on.

My wife has three. One she wore as a schoolgirl in the 1930s; the second, like a pith helmet with a vibrant technicolour band, she bought in Aspen, Colorado, in 1986; and the third, she purchased on Mykonos in 1961. The vendor presented her with a sprig of basil and sewed a chinband onto it to prevent it from blowing away in the wind.

I must have about four, but only two ever really see the light of day. Both were made by an engaging hatter called George Malyard who used to run a small shop off Carnaby Street at the close of the 1960s.

When the sartorial fripperies of that era collapsed in the recession of the 1970s, he emigrated to Australia, and I often wonder what happened to him in that robust country. But I still treasure his hats.

Both are broad-brimmed, inspired by Cecil Beaton. One is of pale yellow straw, elegant enough to be worn in the city, sporting a band of cream petersham; the other is of a looser weave of darker straw, with a brown trim to the brim. Well, it was once brown but is now a pale beige, bleached through years of exposure to the beating rays of the sun.

And what travels those hats have had, in the main through the cities and countryside of northern Italy. As the years pass, they have assumed the status of much-loved friends. Few articles of dress stay the course of a lifetime, but a straw hat is one of them.

MEETING POINTS

∽∾

RICHMOND, Yorkshire, has always been one of my favourite towns. There it sits in the middle of the dales, at first glance looking as though it had been assembled from a cardboard kit for a child. Everything that the ideal Georgian town should have is there, but in miniature: gracious houses, a theatre, assembly rooms, even a winding promenade affording picturesque views. It needs tidying up a bit and there are just a few too many insensitive supermarkets in the central square, but then its inhabitants have to live in the real world.

Strolling through on a golden summer's evening brought nothing but delight. At last we managed to get into the theatre, built in 1788, which had hitherto always been closed. It is so small, really just a large room, but it had boxes and a gallery and a raked stage with grooves for scenery change. We also got into the assembly rooms, equally minute, because someone had left the town hall door open. As a result we had to be shepherded out of a council meeting, but no matter.

What struck me most was what a monument it was to the eighteenth-century creed, 'the pursuit of happiness'. Here a Norman hilltop fortress encircled by a few meandering streets of shops and houses was transformed to meet the social impulses of a new age. In the season the local gentry could reside in elegant houses in the new classical style. There would have been plays in the theatre and music and dancing in the assembly rooms. And, during the day, shops to visit and the promenade along which to parade. But oh, how modest it all was!

AUTUMN

AUTUMN is the orchard. Apple trees epitomizing centuries of cultivation, will if we are lucky be bent down with fruit. From 'Pitmaston Pineapple' to 'Lord Lambourne' it must all be gathered in, either to be stored for use later, or to feed the apple steamer. I think, too, of the pretty fruit of the crabs, 'Golden Hornet' and 'John Downie' above all, and of the claret leaves of the liquidambar and the vines clambering up the house and garden temple. There's the second flush of roses, the Michaelmas daisies, autumn crocus and cyclamen, and then it is all over. The berries and hips on the *Viburnum opulus*, the pyracanthas and rugosas have been taken by the birds before we have had time to enjoy them.

Thereafter it is all retrenchment. There is that Betjemanesque 'nip in the air', and then the first frost comes. In with the agapanthus, causing us to retreat from conservatory to dining room to eat. In, too, with the garden furniture and hose; on, also, with the heating and the Aga. Every year three events chart the progress of this season. The nostalgia of the Last Night of the Proms always brings the curtain down finally on what we think of as summer. Next comes the departure of the house martins. For weeks we watch them practising for the great journey south, diving and swooping from their nests beneath the eaves. And then one day we wake up to find them gone. Lastly, the leaves of the walnut tree close to the house turn a glory of pale yellow, and then, and just as suddenly, we look out one morning to see the

tree bare, the victim of the first severe frost which is winter's punctuation mark.

Autumn Beckons

∽

Autumn began early. By the second week of August, leaves on the beech hedges had begun to brown and crumple. We glimpsed the cyclamen already in flower beneath the cedar, and the berries of the *Malus sargentii* were all too quickly turning from green to bright red. My birthday on August the twenty-third usually signals the advent of autumn. The custom is to take a bottle to the garden and sit in what we call the V & A Temple in the twilight, enjoying the long vista. The seasonal change is often heralded by my wife reaching for her shawl. But that nip in the air has already struck. I was told by a beekeeper that the drones had been frantically busy six weeks before time, signalling a bad winter.

On Eating Alfresco

ఌ

Now that the evenings are drawing in, it is farewell to an innovation which gave us the greatest pleasure: dining alfresco. That, to us, was the only plus side of the relentless heat of the past months; for the first time in almost twenty years of living in the country, eating out of doors night after night became the norm and not an exception.

It ceased to be how one remembers it of old, a dramatic and unusual decision boldly taken, with a long list of consequences in terms of organization and fetching and carrying. Instead, a capacious basket stood on the kitchen floor, in which everything we needed was permanently stacked, cutlery, glasses, candlesticks, table linen and the wine cooler.

It became a wonderful opportunity to create a table composition with all those folk-print tablecloths and boldly patterned ceramics in primary colours that we had accumulated over the years on our travels in Italy and Spain, each one a happy memory of a place and an encounter, notwithstanding the agony of carrying the stuff home and packing it wrapped in bundles of laundry. So a single dinner would include places as far apart as Urbino and Toledo.

We invariably ate later, never before nine, by which time we were in the cool, fading light. My wife had given me the table as a birthday present a few years back, a round ceramic one, seemingly Doulton 1885, but actually China 1985. It and the stools that accompanied it have the virtue of being sturdy enough to be left out for the whole year.

It was a joy to indulge in an almost wholly Mediterranean cuisine with its simple, hearty ingredients: the first course an artichoke, or slices of mozzarella and tomato with basil; a main dish of pasta, a vehicle for lots of home-made sauces, and a salad; with *frutta fresca* or a home-made ice cream as a finale. Dark green olive oil was used in abundance, and local Italian wines washed it all down.

To be conscious of happiness in life is rare. Generally we perceive it in retrospect, but not on these occasions. The fact that it was dark by the time we finished obscured the drought-stricken garden, and we were aware only of the stars dappling the night sky, the balmy warmth of the air, and the opaque shapes of the hedges and trees in varying shades of grey-green into black as our backcloth. But, now the tremulous first chill of autumn is upon us, the dinner basket has had to be dismantled and put into store until next summer.

WILTSHIRE SIBYL

❧

ON a booklist recently, my wife spotted a book by Edith Olivier, with illustrations by Rex Whistler. *Night Thoughts of a Country Landlady* did not ring any bells, and we bought it for the illustrations. I had been fascinated by the author ever since she posthumously entered my life via Cecil Beaton, decades ago, as a kind of salon queen of between-the-wars Wiltshire. The illustrations were, of course, a delight and well worth the £7, but the text went on to stir much more, for its subtitle was 'Being the Pacific Experiences of Miss Emma Nightingale in Time of War'.

The book was published in 1943, and Miss Nightingale is but a thin veil for Miss Olivier and her journals of village life in those years. The lodgers she depicts are her friends, and the soldier 'painter torn from his easel' who painted caricatures of his comrades as Roman legionaries, could only ever be Rex. But it is the picture of the impact of evacuees that is most haunting, bus-loads of London children each clutching a gas mask and a pathetic bundle of belongings.

I was only four in 1939, and too young to be among them, but my brothers were not. Miss Olivier's reflection – after staying at Hardwick, Chatsworth and Haddon in the last summer before the outbreak of war – that 'those stately homes will never quite come back' was to be a devastatingly accurate prediction. And yet there was still time for the eternities of country life: she noted, for instance, that the beech leaves remained golden on the bough until early December in 1942.

FORCED LABOUR

֍

HAVING mapped out a baroque parterre (inspired by one at Het Loo) on the far side of what we still refer to as 'the field', I turned my mind to the garden nearest the house. It is called the Yew Garden for the simple reason that a yew hedge, now nine feet high, was planted to form it in 1974. Anyone who gardens knows that there is always one section that is never quite right. Even with what was there when we came obliterated, it still seems not to belong to us.

Rooms within a house can have that feeling years after occupation. I still sit in the bath, for instance, and think 'This is not mine', despite redecoration and a plethora of pictures and *objets*. The Yew Garden has had an awful history of beds cut and recut, of box hedging unwittingly killed off by one of our well-intentioned, part-time gardeners, who rightly refuse to cement down any of the ornaments there, knowing that I will move them yet again. And now a formal group of four standard euonymus has been ruined by the demise of one, through drought.

There is nothing for it but to replan yet again, a project fired by the arrival of labour from the city in the form of a gardenless, garden-loving flat-dweller. I know of quite a few people who shamelessly exploit such guests, issuing them with a fork and trug practically on arrival. I wrote telling him to bring old clothes, and my wife gave him a new pair of gardening gloves on the first day.

I got him out, skimming off the turf and wheeling it away by the barrowload like some Egyptian slave involved in building a pyramid. 'I'm not in such good condition as you are,' he said, leaning exhausted on his spade, with the sweat pouring off him. 'Don't worry,' I said. 'Just keep going. You'll soon pick up.' I tried to suppress the guilty thoughts crossing my mind. Well, we shall know in the spring, when the planned block plantings of hundreds of tulips into new, box-edged beds burst into bloom, whether our 'slave' ought to be asked back to admire his own handiwork.

'VIE DE BOHÈME'

ལལ⌖ལ

WHEN I spotted a ten-day tour covering some twenty Bohemian and Moravian country houses in Czechoslovakia, I grabbed at it. We would never have got to them on our own, let alone coped with the language problems.

Rarely have I experienced such a revelation of things unknown to me, assailing my retina in a phantasmagoria of delight. Let me tell of just one house which has become one of some dozen houses and castles returned to the Lobkowicz family.

We stood gazing at the remains of what was once a ravishing baroque-into-rococo house, with pretty flanking pavilions enclosing a gracious courtyard. We stared unbelievingly across a sea of tangled undergrowth. The once-smooth white and ochre exterior walls were crumbling away, the windows and shutters either broken or shattered, and a sinister line of damp was running across the façade. Inside, we saw gutted, abandoned rooms, the floorboards ripped out. In the library, the doors of the bookcases had been savaged, and exquisite nests of drawers wantonly bashed.

Dust, filth, muck, was everywhere, and yet within nestled one of the finest sets of small rococo painted and plasterwork rooms I have ever seen: a sequence in faded rose, bleached lemon, pale blue and white with *capriccio vedute* in grey, beige and green, held together with delicate floral swags and garlands. Sacheverell Sitwell and Oliver Messel would have wept to have seen it. I found the tears coming, too, but for a different reason.

Princess Lobkowicz put a brave face on it. The state hands back the house to the descendants of the owners who had it in 1948, but gives them no incentive to restore it: no grants, no remission of tax. Nor are they allowed to sell any of the contents to raise capital for restoration, that is, if they can locate them. The princess spends much time driving around the repositories of country house contents, established by the Communist regime, identifying her property. When she gets pieces back they are divided into groups: instant display, easy restoration, and 'one day'.

Later, we saw another of the family's houses, Roudnice nad Laben, larger than Buckingham Palace and now an academy of military music. The hope is to raise money to create an Institute for Central European

Studies. We walked through desecrated rooms chopped into cubicles, and a great baroque hall, massacred horizontally this time, and heard how soldiers had thrown the library down into the courtyard to be burnt, and how a priest who had protested had suffered the same fate. It was a depressing experience, and I realized how fortunate we have been in this country to escape such a cataclysm.

BOHEMIAN WAYSIDES

ON that Czechoslovakian tour, another great joy was the verges. In the middle of nowhere the bus would stop so that we could clamber out and look at them. On either side, vast fields stretched to the horizon, filled with corn, potatoes and rape gone to seed, but the foreground story was different. The roads were lined with apples and crab apples and the broad swathe of grass beneath was dappled with at least twenty varieties of wildflowers. There were pale violet geraniums, deep pink dianthus, cow parsley, purple campanula, lupins, yellow fennel, sorrel, knapweed and tall spikes of buttery verbascum. Such delight was tempered by the sobering realization of what has vanished from our own country lanes within memory.

MR TOAD

EACH evening we open the back porch door to call in the Reverend Wenceslas Muff. Not that he stays in much longer than to contemplate us safely tucked up in bed, before drifting off again. However, for the last few weeks this nightly event has been attended by a crackling noise, rather like cornflakes being shaken from a packet, coming from the old beech leaves which still lie on the drive, caught up in the *Cotoneaster horizontalis* which threatens to obliterate it.

One evening, out of it ambled Mr Toad. He could not have appeared at a more apposite time, for Alan Bennett had not long since been entrancing us with his reading of *The Wind in the Willows* on Radio 4.

Our Mr Toad was angular, large and brown, and moved with characteristic, crab-like awkwardness towards us. Poor thing, it must have been a terrible summer for him, one of unremitting sunshine and drought, and somewhere beneath that cotoneaster and the adjacent drystone wall there must have been a lovely damp niche in which to pass the daytime before emerging in the cool of darkness.

We did not know quite what to give Mr Toad, so we sprinkled him with the rose of the watering can just to give him a *frisson* of hope, and put a plastic *cachepot* of water down, wishing him 'Good night'.

GIVERNY

∽∾

THE greatest change in our garden has been the extension of the flowering season. This was the outcome of a visit to the painter Monet's garden at Giverny in late August. As it was a garden only ever intended for a few people, we were glad that our party was rattling the gate when it opened on the dot of ten o'clock. So seductively beautiful had it looked in the pictures in garden books that I thought it could only fall short of expectations. But, no, it did not. It was not the water garden that hit me – I have always found those acres of canvas with waterlilies a bore – but the flower garden.

Here were oceans of bloom, sprawling across the paths, rising in serried ranks from lowest to highest in the borders, and then soaring upwards, garlanding their winged way across arches and arbours, seemingly into the empyrean. And here was colour as I had forgotten it could be – neither violent and crude, nor insipid and effete, but keenly vibrant: pinks and yellows, reds and mauves, ochres and oranges thrown together pell-mell. Heleniums, asters, helianthemums, rudbeckias, dahlias, Japanese anemones and roses seemed to chorus to each other in joy.

And now, as a result of this ecstasy, I have a touch of Giverny in my flower garden. The yellows and purples ascend, succeeding the paler tints of summer: primrose into lemon into buttercup, and on by progression through the autumnal spectrum to the imperial hue. I suppose the result to anyone else's eyes is just another end-of-season herbaceous border, but for me it is the keyhole through which I glimpse Monet's floral paradise.

NEWS-ANCE

∽∽∽∽

SOME friends of ours never take a newspaper, nor do they have a television set; their only contact with the greater world is a wireless permanently tuned to Radio 3, which reduces news to a minimum. I have a sympathy with this approach to life when I think of all the years of misspent passion consumed in the politics of art. In our case, the *Today* programme is still firmly turned on as I shave, and also while we breakfast, and two daily papers are duly looked through on delivery. But more and more comes the moment with the radio when one says, 'Switch it off, I just can't bear it anymore', or, in the case of the newspapers, I just let them pile up and whisk through them a week later.

Earlier in the year, I remarked to an Italian friend on the fact that the government had fallen again in Rome. 'Oh, that,' he said. 'What does that matter. Let them get on with it. We prefer to live and create.' It was a comment which has increasingly given me cause for thought: how to reclaim the larger part of one's life from being a constant slave to instant news.

On the shelves in my writing room are the books I am using at present, whole worlds filling my day with adventures of the mind. And every day, too, there are the pleasurable incidents of domestic life, from a geranium flowering for the first time in the conservatory, to Muff asking to be towelled down after the rain. And from my window both garden and countryside ply their eternal way, oblivious of the pain of perpetual news, reminding me of a fairer balance in the bestowal of one's time and mind.

VICTORIAN AGAPANTHUS

∽∾∽

THE size and intensity of colour of the agapanthus flowerheads have been quite extraordinary: feathery balls of deepest hyacinth blue atop a stem arising from a shaft of succulent leaves. Each day, as evening comes on, they seem to acquire a luminosity. We do not know what variety they are; they are certainly not hardy, for the first frost signals the major operation of moving these huge terracotta containers into the safety of the garden room for the winter.

They do, however, have an interesting pedigree, for we can trace them back to the 1890s, when their forebears adorned the terrace of Frewin Hall, the country house right in the middle of Oxford where my wife's grandfather, Sir Charles Oman, lived. From there they descended to my in-laws in Putney, where they multiplied so prolifically that many of them ended up being potted into old oil cans painted green. It was in those unaesthetic containers that we inherited them, and piecemeal began to repot them.

That is a horrible task. It involves getting a hacksaw to the roots of the plants – that is if you can ever get them out of the container in the first place. One literally saws through them. This major operation is required about every decade, and is an occasion when plant-loving friends must be alerted to the imminence of pieces for them.

I know of no other blue in the garden quite like the blue of these agapanthus, and when I look on them I like to imagine the safe world in which they originated. Who knows but that they were not admired by Lewis Carroll or Max Beerbohm in some sunshine idyll of lace parasols and straw boaters?

CAT PATRON

∾

'YOU'RE a patron of the Cat Protection League, aren't you?' the nurse said. Being in hospital in the aftermath of an operation I felt cornered. I could not deny it, and certainly the Reverend Wenceslas Muff would have ticked me off on my return home if I had. For some reason I have never fathomed, cats have been drawn to me, like some kind of mobile mecca, ever since childhood. These late summer months have been filled with what I can only describe as a series of bitter-sweet tales of love and loss such as only the cat and dog lover knows.

The nurse's tale began with a sad mission, upon which I counselled, to rescue what seemed to be a stray cat, pathetically ill and starved, which she at last located sitting in a heap in an orchard. She rang the doorbell of the neighbouring house, hoping to be allowed to sweep the cat away to safety, only to be put in her place by the owner, who said that the poor creature was perfectly well. Rebuffed, the nurse visited the local cat shelter and took home a delectable minute white bundle of fur with a black splodge on its face, which had been found in a dustbin.

Next came the saga of Titus, who had been run over and was discovered by his owner under a shrub in the garden. He was whisked off to the vet and put on a drip. When he returned home, his sister, Audrey, stared at him with the lustrous feline eyes of disbelief, but he was soon able to hobble upstairs and I last heard of them entwined asleep together. I sent him a get-well card from Muff.

Two happy endings, but there was a third not so. A friend rang from New England to tell us that Bobby was no more, having given his mistress warning, by attempting to make that solitary final voyage into a nearby wood, which leaves any cat lover shattered. As I write this, Muff is stretched out beside me on the garden bench, purring, and I think how lucky we are still to have him.

HORTICULTURAL HEROINES

∽

THE world of gardening is peopled by remarkable women. On a recent short visit to France we visited two such, Madame Mallet and Princess Sturdza. Both preside over extraordinary gardens in the Dieppe area. Reign might perhaps be an apter word, for both exude a mixture of dignified regal graciousness combined with the common touch. The Princess, her hair tucked into a headscarf, wields a tri-pronged implement like a trident, warning her visitors that one foot on a bed would attract a light bash, and repetition, something akin to amputation.

A respectful silence fell. Well it might, for this Norwegian, married to a Romanian prince, must be compost queen of France. She scours the locality for fallen leaves. Every plant is given its special winter blanket and, as a result, is twice the normal size. We sat beneath the trees in a small orchard and had tea, my wife explaining her own compost cult, which included even orange peel. 'Don't,' the Princess screamed, 'you will poison your plants – unless you scrub every orange free of its chemical sprays.'

Madame Mallet's realm at Moutiers was a Lutyens house, a minor masterpiece whose contents had been looted in two wars. The decision to return was hers, as were those to recreate the Jekyllesque garden and the acres of woodland planting, which stretched down to the coast, and which Monet had painted. We strolled through the undulating terrain, the trees rising from drifts of hydrangeas of a strange, incandescent blue. Madame Mallet, splendid in her eighties, her straw hat perched squarely on her head, strode on, telling the tale, seemingly indomitable and thinking still of tomorrow. 'Revolutions come and go and you must accept them,' she mused, 'but life has to go on.'

The Lady Vanishes

∾⌇∾

THE slump in farming hit Herefordshire badly. Farmers'
wives banded together to establish a *cordon bleu* circuit
of farmhouses for visitors, who were passed from one
gastronomic feast to the next. Suitable itineraries were
fleshed out, enabling them to appreciate the delights of
this county to the full.

All this came to my notice when I was asked to act as
the Herefordshire host in a televised programme that
would explore the county as a tourist area of some
potential. There is something both beguiling and manic
about everything to do with television. It demands,
and exacts, top gear — torrents of adrenaline projected
through every pore from the moment the camera rolls.
All those takes and retakes. All those re-enactments of
the same encounter again and again from different angles
for even the simplest of programmes. And then the
pauses for the sun to reappear, or the aeroplane to pass
over.

We were lucky. On the whole, the countryside
looked a dream. A bright journalist was cast as the
itinerant visitor, but quickly found herself reduced to the
role of a stage walk-on, staring with wide-eyed wonder
as we hared from Abbey Dore to Llanbedr, recalling
everyone from the Lord Scudamore of the apples to the
Reverend Mr Kilvert of the diaries. Sadly, our shooting
at Bacton had to be abandoned. Yes, the vicar said, the
church had recently been rewired, but when we got
there, what was missing was a three-pronged plug.

So the viewers did not see one of my favourite local sites, the memorial to Elizabeth I's lady of the privy chamber, Blanche Parry. Here queen and servant kneel, facing each other, in a church on a remote hilltop, with its moving verse, plucked from the heart of Tudor England, in which this sturdy Welshwoman recalls her great mistress 'Whose cradell saw I rockte'.

MARIGOLDS

༄

WE had been gathering the seedheads from the marigolds before the greedy finches made off with them. There were still a few brilliant flowerheads left, adding to the final autumn haze of golds, oranges and purples which signals the finale of the floral year. I find it astonishing how much pleasure we have had from these humble flowers.

My wife always sows the seeds of several varieties in the kitchen garden in spring. Then, in late May and June, comes the moment when they cry out for transplanting. This year, in a rare moment of horticultural economy, I seized upon them to scatter amid the Hidcote lavender and rue in the box-edged beds of the Rose Garden. The result was pure enchantment. Their many shades of ochre, honey yellow, citrus orange, peach, tangerine and apricot gold were dappled through the cooling washes of the lavender's grey and the rue's steely blue foliage. And, for a period, there was the electric effect of their contrast with the deep purple spikes of the lavender. As for those left in the kitchen garden, they lightened the stormiest of summer days, peppered among the many greens of the produce.

There is something deeply satisfying about a flower that is part of history, was known to Chaucer and Shakespeare, and still gives such delight. For medieval man even to look on marigolds, we are told, would draw 'evil humours', and 'maidens make garlands of it when they go to feasts or bridals because it hath fair yellow flowers and ruddy'. John Gerard, the Elizabethan herbalist, describes a wonderful variety called 'Jackanapes-on-horsebacke . . . for this plant doth bring forth at the top of the stalke one floure like the other marigolds, from which start forth sundry other smal floures, yellow likewise and of the same fashion as the first . . .' Sitting one evening in the Rose Garden, I fell that I should have liked to have been joined by him so that we could have shared our experiences of this humble, serviceable, but most lovely of old-fashioned flowers.

TODAY'S AUTOLYCUS

∾∾

ONE of the problems about country living is the pedlars. After twenty years, we have established a tic-tac system with a neighbour, signalling to each other the imminence of the next unwanted itinerant. Of these, one in particular heads the list. Twice a year a decrepit vehicle disgorges an untidy figure who calls at the back door. It is usually my wife who answers it.

The exchange begins with, 'Can I speak to the man of the house?' Anything more likely to rouse Dr Oman's hackles than this sexist question it would be difficult to think of. Firmly rebuffed, the fellow nonetheless continues to hector us before offering his services to tarmac the drive. The fact that he has been told times without number that we do not want it done, and that if we did, we would use a builder of our own choice, makes no impression upon him. After a disagreeable and just short of threatening exchange, he goes, and the next visit is awaited. The neighbour who is similarly bothered, and whose house is hidden at the bottom of a winding half-mile drive in a cul-de-sac, goes through a similar, if more unbelievable, exchange. 'What are you doing here?' elicits the reply, 'I just happened to be passing.'

FREEZER FRENZY

SEPTEMBER tends to be a race against time, trying to cope with the onrush of ripe fruit from the orchard. We began in August with our own peaches – quite a triumph – no fewer than fifty. From these came juice with which we made ice cream, as well as purée for *membrilo*. Then followed the plums. A gorgeous sight is a plum tree with its branches bent earthwards under the sheer weight of its fruit. I wish that I could say that I warmed quite as much to the sight of them gathered into large plastic buckets sitting on the surface of the kitchen work counter.

There can be few more dreary tasks than stoning a mountain of plums which then have to be cooked, scattered with cinnamon and doused in clear honey, in relays in the oven. After they are cooked they have to be batched up in serried ranks of plastic containers, each labelled P, and thence to the inevitable deep-freeze.

That labelling has its dangers, for we moved on next to pears, which came our way quite by accident, due to a branch falling off a neighbour's tree. Very important not to label those containers P too, I thought. Pears embody a different kind of boredom – peeling. This is a task only relieved by having the radio on, and fortunately the Proms playing – Prokofiev and pears, as it happened. Into a huge earthenware crock they go, to be sunk beneath an ocean of red wine (I hope consumers never guess at its inferiority), along with cinnamon, cloves and sugar. And then there is a bonus, because they get pushed into the Aga overnight to emerge next morning mahogany-coloured.

ORGANIC ORGY

YOUNG organizations exude a brio which is deeply attractive, and so it was with the Henry Doubleday Research Association at Ryton-on-Dunsmore near Coventry. Despite its leaflet trumpeting that it was 'the largest organic organization in Europe', there was something pleasantly modest about the enterprise. Enthusiasm was everywhere, and there was no feeling of being ensnared into hard sell but of a silent conversion to a cause through example. Shop and restaurant were simple wooden structures, and even the loo turned out to be portable. The various demonstration areas were punched out of field turf almost haphazardly. This was certainly no design paradise.

But what appealed was its honesty: onions were drying off in the sun on the metal interior of an old sofa; bits of decaying carpet were cut to encircle cabbages. Everywhere we were encouraged to touch and experience, not just the fragrant herbs, but the contents of the plastic compost containers by lifting and poking them. The demonstration kitchen garden – one half with produce sky high on compost, the other soil-bound through lack of nourishment – said everything. I now understood why my wife had returned from a visit and set to with shredder, a packet of QR compost accelerator, sheets of black plastic and old car tyres.

Like all the best ideas, the organization's is a simple one. I really wish that I had seen something like it twenty years ago when I began. It banishes all garden mystique and aims at utter accessibility. So far unique, one of these is needed within reach of everyone in every part of the country.

WARTIME MEMORIES

AT this time of year, too, going away for even a short time will signal a glut of produce from the kitchen garden. While we are in the United States, the tomatoes will ripen, and as quickly rot; so in order not to lose the crop, we make chutney. For both my wife and myself that operation always signals memories of the Second World War, and those endless radio exhortations that we must win on the kitchen front as well as on the battlefield.

I was brought up in a 1920s terrace house in the suburbs of north London, and some of my earliest memories are of the front garden given over to produce, with rows of tomatoes, neatly staked and tied, burgeoning beneath the bay window. As soon as there was the first hint of frost, the green tomatoes would be taken indoors to ripen, mostly on windowsills. We were always awash with them, and my mother made quantities of chutney. This was used to enliven cold meat from the weekly joint, which had to meander its existence through more days than I care to remember.

And when Julia began her chutney-making, the main recipe she used came out of an old Ministry of Agriculture and Fisheries publication. No glossy plates or beguiling wood engravings, but pages of solid text in an earnest format. Soon the whole house was engulfed in the pungent aroma of malt vinegar as the brew simmered in the large conserving pan, and before long there was the satisfying sight of jars filled, capped and neatly labelled in the store cupboard.

Green-tomato sauce will be made next, but I have promised not to repeat a green-tomato pie I once made.

John Taylor's Monument

In the centre of the Rose Garden stands an urn which came from my wife's aunt's house, Bride Hall, near Welwyn in Hertfordshire. Lady Lenanton, or Carola Oman as she was better known, always referred to it as 'John Taylor's Monument', and we did not fathom the reason until she died. Then the urn came to us, and the slab upon which it had rested was found to be inscribed in memory of a John Taylor who had died in 1821.

Although the urn at once found a home as the culmination of a vista, that headstone was to migrate from site to site for more than a decade. At last, this

autumn, it has come to rest. A new path leads to a landing before the descent towards the Rose Garden. Every visitor pauses at this point to drink in the panorama, and it is beneath their feet that John Taylor has come to his final repose. When I asked my wife how we were to explain his presence, she replied: 'We will tell people that tradition has it that he was the builder of the house!'

This England

∽

VISITING the marvellous exhibition at the National Gallery, centred on the Wilton Diptych, I was fascinated by the discovery that the sphere at the top of the banner held by an angel has England as the verdant island set in a silver sea. How strangely potent that mysterious image remains after all these centuries – the legend of the sacrosanct island girt by stormy waters – whether celebrated by Virgil, Shakespeare, Purcell or Thomas Arne. Not even the noble vision of Europe can erode its powerful and haunting beauty, or its hold on the British imagination.

POTATO MUSEUM

THE great taste experience of the year from the kitchen garden has been the exotic potato varieties we have grown, supplied by Mrs M. Maclean, châtelaine of the potato museum in Perthshire. Some of the varieties come from a group categorized as the 'Museum Collection Pack', of which the buyer is allowed but three tubers of each kind.

Of these, I recall with pleasure 'Doon Pearl' for its handsome shape and indeed pearly flesh, and 'Mauve Queen' for its skin of translucent aubergine. Two other varieties from the same source were likewise consumed with a reverence not normally accorded to the humble potato. 'Salad Blue' really did have azure flesh, and 'Purple Congo', billed as a 'curiosity', lived up not only to that billing, but to the fact that it was a poor cropper. Three tubers produced four minute potatoes of a deep vinous colour throughout. They were gone in a trice but, I must admit, the memory of them lingers on.

CHASING RAINBOWS

❧

A DOUBLE rainbow crossed the sky as we drove north-wards past Leominster to a meeting of our local branch of the National Council for the Conservation of Plants and Gardens, at Berrington Hall. As we approached the bend in the road towards Henry Holland's chaste neo-classical house, we saw it from afar, framed within a vast rainbow. The radiance of the colour was so intense and seemingly so solid that we felt we could leave the car, and walk on the site from which one side sprang upwards in a nearby field.

It is always moving to find oneself travelling through the reality of the landscape immortalized by our greatest painters. Through a fortuitous combination of lightning showers, shifting clouds, changing patterns of light and the golden, ochre, russet and burnt-orange tints of autumn, we had found ourselves driving through a succession of compositions by Constable.

The meeting was a long one, beginning with a plant-ing of historic Herefordshire apple trees in an abandoned old walled garden, contributing to a living archive of vanished varieties. We arrived late but in time for one of those glorious makeshift picnic lunches in what had been the kitchen of the great house.

Cold weather demands hot food, and although soup and coffee presented no problem, the hot mini quiches did, until my wife hit on the idea of engulfing them in an envelope of foil and bubble plastic, working on the old hay box principle. They emerged steaming.

Looking across the gathering, I was struck by the delightfully disorganized chaos that seems to attend the British picnic — tweed clad figures arising from a sea of paper and plastic. Everyone jovial with an *esprit* a bit like that which unites refugees.

On a dresser to one side there were plates of apples exhibited like the contents of a reliquary tabernacle, among them 'Bess Pool', 'Lady's Finger', 'Ten Commandments' and 'Golden Pippin'. After lunch we all rushed to the plant sale. We returned to find the room had been transformed into a lecture theatre for a talk on Thomas Andrew Knight, to whose enterprise we owed many of these apple varieties.

Such is the compartmentalization of knowledge in our century, that I was unaware that T. A. Knight was the brother of Richard Payne Knight, who equally transformed our landscape, but in a different way, by means of the Picturesque. There must, I thought, have been some interchange between these two brothers but, no, I was firmly told, there was none. I still wonder.

STEAMED-UP

∾⌁∾

MY wife's eccentricity in planting sixty different varieties of historic apple to supply a household of only two ceased to be an indulgence when the Finnish apple-steamer made its appearance. From the earliest windfalls on, the Aga is relit to accommodate this marvellous and commodious contraption, a tiered stainless-steel steamer, in the bottom of which the water quietly simmers, and into the top of which vast quantities of unpeeled, roughly chopped apples are piled, to be reduced to a repulsive brown pulp as they disgorge that pinkish-rose syrup that is pure unadulterated apple juice.

A horrid rubber pipe hangs down on one side, rather like an unresolved umbilical cord, and from this the nectar is periodically released into warm old white-wine bottles and hermetically sealed. These are carefully labelled with the year and the contents, often in code. Q & A, for instance, means quince and apple, which is especially delectable. They then make their way to the top of the cellar steps to descend and be shelved along with the wine. In bumper years we produce bottles by the tree, and compare the juice of 'Charles Ross' with that of 'Arthur Turner'.

THE ORCHARD GHOST

∾⌁∾

IS there a ghost in the orchard? It is not exactly a problem that I thought we would have to cope with, although my wife did see one as a child. The haunting centres on one of the most beautiful of all our historic apple trees, 'Beauty of Bath', whose branches are annually laden with bright shiny red fruit that seems almost incandescent.

It stands, along with its peers, in an enclosure of dark green yew. It is not alone in bearing fruit, for all around the other trees are equally laden – but in no other instance does the fruit suddenly vanish overnight. This is now the third year in succession that on one day we have paused to admire the radiance of the tree, only to awake the next morning to find it empty, not a single apple left on any branch, and yet the rest of the orchard untouched.

On the first occasion this happened we vaguely dismissed the aberration by assigning it to passing gypsies or local children. After two more similar happenings, it can seemingly no longer be so easily explained away and put from the mind. Why that particular tree? Why every single apple gone, leaving it stripped bare? So far we can come up with no logical explanation.

TWENTY YEARS ON

∾✧∾

WE have lived in the country now for nearly twenty years – not long, it must be admitted, and certainly we will go to the grave as strangers in our beloved adopted county. Looking back over those years, the 1970s epitomized an escape from a beleaguered urban environment. We knew that here we could survive, with our own wood to burn and our own vegetable store to eat. At its bleakest, during a petrol strike, we bought bicycles, now in the loft, to ensure some form of transport.

We lived through the loss of our elm trees, the terrible drought of 1976, and two appalling winters in the early 1980s, years which brought many other changes. Our village shop vanished, Sunday postal services ceased, the local bus service was privatized, and retirement homes sprang up like mushrooms. Drive-in supermarkets arrived on the edges of our local towns, making possible a far more cosmopolitan cuisine. Deep freezes and double glazing proliferated.

Though, even here in remote Herefordshire, the effects of atmospheric pollution began to affect our trees, the renewed prosperity saw even the most dilapidated and squalid cottage or farm outbuilding converted or spruced up. On the whole, *pace* the laments of farmers, our area of the country is in a far better state than it was twenty years ago.

PLANT AID

PLANTING a box and gravel parterre has long been a dream, but it has now become a reality. We decided to site it in the middle of a paved circle of yew, and I painted onto the slabs the flowing baroque pattern which encircled our intertwined initials, J and R. It was left to Wilf to chip out the pattern through the hardcore, and fill the space with earth for the plants – an awful job.

As formal gardens come back into fashion, dwarf box becomes increasingly elusive, but an old friend put me onto a man in a nearby village who had laid out his own box garden, and over the years had rooted hundreds of cuttings from the annual trim. He arrived with beautiful bushy plants, and when I asked him to whom to make out the cheque, he said to the local Methodist Church, towards the repair of the roof. What an enormously pleasant surprise. I shall never be able to look at the parterre without calling to mind that church, saved just a little from ruin by my horticultural folly and the grower's inspired generosity.

GOING OUT WITH A BANG

∽∽∽

WE had been bidden to a pyrotechnic display and the unveiling of a headstone – an unlikely alliance, but, as we knew the daughter of those who lay beneath the stone, we crossed country one autumn Sunday morning in expectation of we knew not what.

Our destination was not that far – only seemingly so, for the tiny church at Fawley was caught high up in a bend of the Wye, bestowing on this piece of landscape a remoteness that belied the reality.

We drove up a track and were waved to a parking space in a farmyard. Mercifully, the rain held off as we joined the throng trudging towards the small graveyard around the tiny Norman church which, on first encounter, seemed no more than a barn.

The scene we encountered came as a complete

surprise, for there, in comfortable, country clothes, friends gathered, jostling and chattering, as others with capacious baskets on their arms threaded their way through, bearing glasses and bottles of wine – kindling a party atmosphere.

The greensward before us was punctuated by recent graves. In the middle rose a vertical feature draped in black velvet, from which stretched lines to Roman candles attached along the fence behind, with rockets stationed at intervals crossing the grass beyond. Those we had gathered to honour, who lay in the warm embrace of the red earth of Herefordshire, had loved to set ablaze the night sky with fireworks. Now, we had gathered to witness the unveiling of their memorial.

At a given moment we were bidden to arrange ourselves in a semi-circle beneath the branches of the ancient trees. Then two touchpapers were lit, whose trail triggered off rockets in succession as it moved towards the fence. One by one they crashed and cracked into the grey sky until, in a trice, the whole length of the fencing was a glory of Roman candles, roaring, sizzling, and, with a mighty wham, the black velvet pall whooshed heavenwards, revealing the bronze headstone. The tomb was engulfed by a theatrical swirl of smoke, and that was it.

We stood exhilarated and stunned, like those in the aftermath of a sudden storm. It was a strange, eccentric and oh so English occasion, with a mad wild pyrotechnic poetry of its own. That it could happen at all, or that such a beautiful headstone could be placed, was due, I learned, to the graveyard somehow being outside normal ecclesiastical jurisdiction. That fact in itself was food for thought, on an occasion which it would be hard to match for touching beauty and imagination.

ISAAC NEWTON'S FAVOURITE FRUIT

NOVEMBER is the time of year when that most delectable of orchard fruits, the quince, is to be gathered into baskets and brought into the kitchen. Gleaming yellow-gold in colour, they scent the air with their honey-sweet fragrance. My wife has a passion for them, and no fewer than ten trees are dotted through the garden.

Two are what might be described as 'family' being descendants of the tree at her grandfather's house, Frewin Hall, in Oxford. Erasmus is said to have visited the house, and I always liked to imagine that our quinces dated back to Tudor England when this fruit was highly prized. But two years ago the tree was identified as Serbian from Lescovata, which put paid to that romantic notion.

We have two more of the old Portugal variety, which Parkinson in his *Paradisi in Sole* describes as 'a great yellow Quince . . . this is so pleasant being fresh gathered that it may be eaten like unto an Apple without offense'. I have never attempted to consume one raw, as quinces are a tough fruit, but that is beside the point. Their intriguing flavour gives a culinary lift to any apple dish. With pears, too, they make a marvellous compote, or even on their own, when they turn a delicate vinous

autumn tint. At the moment Julia is busy making a Portuguese *membrilo* as well as quince jelly, whose translucent amber beauty makes it a special gift for any receiver.

I always seize the best unimpaired quinces for baking what Jane Grigson described as Sir Isaac Newton's favourite pudding. Stuffed with caster sugar and butter, and stood in a little water, they emerge in an hour or so, soft and delicious, to perfume the dining room and heighten anticipation of their consumption with cold cream. Perhaps it was a quince and not an apple which, legend has it, fell on that famous head.

TIME CHANGE

THE change of the clocks, which also symbolizes the arrival of winter, always traumatizes me. The only other part of the year which has a similar power to engender an immovable introspective melancholy is between the aftermath of Christmas and New Year's Eve. There one is caught, haunted by a meditation on the old year's failures and, as yet, un-uplifted by the promise of the new.

From those days there is no escape, but from a government-instituted mandatory time change there is. That, mercifully, is eventually, we are told, to be phased out as we bring ourselves more and more into line with the rest of Europe. No more turning one's watch backwards and forwards as the plane touches down.

The autumnal time change is by far the most depressing. 'Spring forward, fall back' is the old saying to cling to, but the latter is always a dismal injunction for the change in the rhythm of one's day is so fundamental. No longer the happiness of cutting down the herbaceous plants or tidying up the vegetable garden in the fading light – a precious period gone, treasured as a treat to be looked forward to after hours spent staring at the word processor. On one day this seems just possible and on the next it has gone. Winter does not creep up on one, as I feel it should in the country. It arrives like a thunderclap turning us overnight into inward- and not outward-looking beings.

GARDEN TO JARDIN

∽∾∾∾

THE Château de Courson lies to the south of Paris, in the Ile de France. On being asked to sign copies of the French editions of my garden design books there, I naturally looked up the place in Michel Racine's admirable recent *Guide des Jardins de France*, to find that it was a garden laid out by Berthault, who was responsible for Josephine's Malmaison, and that twice a year it played host to a horticultural event. I was obviously destined to be some part of that, I concluded.

We stepped out of the taxi one late autumn Saturday morning to be practically knocked over by a bustling cavalcade of French families out for the day, and bearing plants – in some cases, large trees – towards their waiting cars. I do not think that the recent French garden renaissance had ever been more vivid to me than in this scene.

Patrice Fustier, the château owner, explained how they had begun in 1983 with only three stalls, and that now, some ten years on, it had taken on the atmosphere of a nascent Chelsea. Not quite, for it had a delectable fresh amateur pell-mell about it. What it lacked in finish, it more than made up for in enthusiasm and *joie de vivre*.

The stalls and booths sprawled their way across the grass at the back of the château. One had a wonderful range of oak trees; another, all the apples grown in the Ile de France (not a 'Golden delicious' in sight); a third, a range of roses which included ones rediscovered in the gardens of old châteaux. Two British nurseries had piled their wares into lorries and ferried them across the Channel, plying their business in French as bad as mine.

That I found enterprising, and it was particularly good that one of them had brought decorative trellis made by a firm having a hard time in this country because of the recession.

In a rambling outbuilding there was a splendid display of garden books; not all, I am glad to say, translated from the English and exporting updated Gertrude Jekyll. Indeed, I was struck by how many new French books were appearing, and how garden history and restoration were burgeoning.

The sun shone and lit up the parkland, dappling this happy setting, which had an atmosphere uniquely its own. I can see that we shall soon have to look to our gardening laurels. And about time, too.

THE BLUES

༄

I SUPPOSE anyone maintaining a house in the country is driven mad by the vagaries of workmen. This was the year of painting the outside – certainly sorely needed, for we were peering at paintwork peeling down to the wood beneath, and chunks of incipient rot. We have a simple principle of concentrating works, so that, instead of endless dislocation strung out over months, there is one concentrated horror.

So, on a certain Monday in August, the builder was to

come to repoint a chimney, a plumber and an electrician for the kitchen, and the painter. Everything went according to plan – except for the painter. No amount of telephoning, not even a telegram could elicit a response. 'Oh yes,' said the person who recommended him, 'he does take rather a lot of holidays.'

It made me wonder what the effect would have been if I had conducted my life in this way. No matter, there was no alternative but to face a second dislocation in the late autumn, when the weather is wet, and this we have done. There was to have been an excitement about it, for we were thinking of painting the house blue, inspired by blue-green *treillage* in Dutch and French gardens and a recent visit to Hidcote, where we noticed that much of the house was blue, and garden gates, too.

In the end, however, we lost our nerve and tamely reverted to pale greys and off-whites, although we did successfully paint two garden seats a green-blue colour.

BELEAGUERED

❧

UNIVERSITIES, like all our great cultural bastions, are having a terribly beleaguered time these days. The last fields to pine for must be those of academe, but as Keele was once generous enough to bestow an honorary doctorate upon me, I was more than happy to give a fund-raising lecture.

I am full of admiration for staff, whose energies ought to be directed towards learning and teaching, having to cope with raising money. I am equally struck by those of the local community who have almost rediscovered their own university and are determined that it shall not sink. It is sad, though, to think that it needed a crisis to engender such a reawakening.

As an evening, it went off like clockwork and was well done. It was good to see the vast Victorian mansion that is Keele's heart brought to life for such an occasion, using in sequence what are magnificent rooms of the period for dinner, lecture and party. There is, however, a fair balance to be kept, and I mused on the never-ending, often hollow occasions of this sort over which I had presided during the Thatcher decade, and pondered whether they had been worth the effort, and was it really the way to keep the flame of civilization burning anyway? If, indeed, it was burning bright, that would be an unanswerable riposte to my doubts, but instead, everywhere I seem to see the flames guttering amid the encroaching gloom.

Still, before I left, there was the sight of the restored garden to gladden me: box-edged parterres in the chill morning sunlight, the compartments glowing with heather ground-cover, and the corners punctuated by elegant yew sentinels, the whole held together by a handsome fountain. Now fund-raising for that was entirely appropriate, but for the basics of a university, well . . .

SWITCH OFF

∾∾∾

I HAVE a theory that the Midlands Electricity Board has a switch which bears the name of our lane, and is immediately turned off on the approach of any meteorological disturbance. Any year is punctuated by sudden blackouts, which accounts for the forest of candlesticks and boxes of matches dotted through the house. We are also the luckless possessors of a junction box on our land, which has blown up in its time.

Recently there was a mighty clap of thunder, a gargantuan crack of lightning, followed by a downpour of hailstones like lead pellets beating against the window-panes. Off the electricity went, plunging the house into the murky half-light of a late autumn afternoon. I rang the breakdown service. Yes, I was told, other houses locally had been cut off. There were, I was warned, difficulties, so we fortified ourselves for the hours to come by stationing the candles at crucial points and praying we would not need to heave the duvets onto the deep-freeze.

I was cooking when the breakdown service arrived as night fell. Out leapt the MEB men. 'Can I check the trip switch,' one asked. A horrible thought slowly began to cross my mind as he made his way to the scullery, flung open the cupboard door and promptly turned the lights on again in a trice. I had rightly been humbled.

AN AMERICAN MASTERPIECE

∽∾

I HAD never been to Dumbarton Oaks before. It is always exhilarating to visit a famous garden that you have known previously only through photographs. You will be familiar with only a few parts of the jigsaw, and certainly oblivious of the relationship of its various parts.

That we came at all was by accident, for I had failed to link giving a lecture at the venerable Folger Shakespeare Library in Washington with the possibility of seeing Beatrix Farrand's masterpiece. But there it was on a glorious autumn afternoon, some ten acres right in the heart of Georgetown, cascading down a hillside. Its scale was quite unexpected, for its many delectable enclosures were small. The changes of level also came as a surprise. Into these few acres the designer, under the aegis of the garden's owners, Mr and Mrs Woods Bliss, had crammed memories of Italian, French and English gardens past and present. But the overall result was unmistakably American.

And that is what I found so refreshing. However grand the effects, American gardens always have a modesty about them, which is deeply appealing. The formal elements quickly give way to small, meandering brick paths of a kind Batty Langley would have loved. There is a delight in native trees planted in such a way that one can savour to the full their fruits and foliage tints. The flaming hues of autumn were incandescent, seeming to bathe the valley in a fiery glow.

Americans love strong colour, but even then the

herbaceous border came as something of a shock, vibrant with russet, yellow, auburn and Titian-hued chrysanthemums unashamedly clashing in front of a background tapestry of violet, lavender and purple Michaelmas daisies set against yew. That glorious effect was achieved in a way that I had not seen done before. All the chrysanthemums were grown in pots and plunged into the border in full flower.

WINTER

WINTER begins when dusk is at five o'clock, when the fountain is turned off and baled, when everyone is made to come in through the back door, for the front one is thick hung with layers against cold and wind. Off with the summer bedding and on with the duvets and electric blanket. Cotton tee-shirts and jeans are washed and folded away in favour of woollens and corduroys.

Late autumn into early winter is an ugly time in the garden: so much pruning, clearing up, sweeping, tidying and bonfires. By January the worst is over, and it could hardly look lovelier: an architectural fantasy in shades of green and brown, an intriguing pattern of shadows in golden sunlight, mysterious in mist or, better still, sparkling under snow or glittering beneath a hoar frost.

Winter, however, is also setting the mousetraps, for into the house mice come, escaping the cold. It is checking the stores, for a fall of snow can cut us off. Baskets of logs must be mustered in the back hall for the fire. Torches, candles and matches have always to be to hand against electricity cuts. My wife gets out her patchwork and I ply my needle, producing yet another rug or cushion. Hibernation sets in, culminating in the period between Christmas and New Year when it seems as though time had stood still. By then the shortest day has gone, but the grimmest months, January and February, lie ahead, lustreless rain-sodden weeks which seem interminable. But end they do when spring proclaims that yet another year of a life in the country is about to begin.

GARDEN PICTURE

∾∿∽

I LOVE the russet leaves of beech hedges in winter. As I type this onto my computer I look down from my book-room window to a really handsome beech enclosure planted about fifteen years ago. Like so much, it started as one thing and developed into another, but now it is the ante-room to the main garden, with a fountain and brick paving as a preface to it.

Downstairs we look out onto this tableau from our breakfast room. Tall dark green Irish yews and glossy-leaved box cones flanking statues are silhouetted before this tapestry of caramel-coloured leaves, and inside its walls there is yew topiary and fruit trees. For winter contentment in the garden I know of nothing to beat this in terms of texture and colour contrast, besides its dramatic response to light.

A COUNTRY LIBRARY

∾∿∽

WINTER months are the ones for reordering the house on days when it is impossible to work outside. A decision to reshelve a library is one taken with short-lived optimism, for the reality of seeing it through to the bitter end is quite another matter. My library opens off my writing room. It is not that large, and very much a working area, with book stacks jutting out from the walls, and the books arranged under subject.

The classification of a private library ought to reflect the structure of the owner's mind, and that inevitably changes over the years. In addition, the best of systems in the end breaks down in the face of bequests and gifts of books; when there is no more room to jam anything in, little heaps start springing up.

Once reshelving starts, there is no going back. It has to be accompanied by the iron will to discard several thousand books in order to re-establish any order. My wife cannot bear parting with anything, and I find that on seeing this massive evacuation, she has hastily constructed makeshift shelves of bricks and old planks in the garden room, to take in the throw-outs which ranged from books in Russian, which I cannot read, to a set of the Waverley novels.

I was still short of space, and so we studied a guest bedroom, which had already sacrificed a bay to take in the sections on contemporary biography and Cecil Beaton, in order to build yet another bookcase. I never mind sleeping in a room jammed with books, and one hopes one's guests will feel the same.

Self-sufficiency, in terms of the civilized life and information, remain the essence of any library in the country, however small. No one can afford to be without a run of the great classics, the odd volume on the peerage, or a handful on local topography, architecture and history.

FORGOTTEN GARDEN

∽৵৩৲৹

A LETTER from nowhere asked me if I would like to see over Holme Lacy, the splended mansion of the Scudamore family. For some reason or other it has always seemed to me a house shrouded in mystery, perhaps of my own invention.

All I knew about it had been culled years before from articles in pre-1914 issues of *Country Life*, which showed gracious interiors with carving by Grinling Gibbons, and rare survivals, such as a raised canal, in its grounds. Years ago, the whole complex passed into the hands of the local authorities, who turned it into a hospital and then, in the 1980s, sold it for development as a country house hotel.

It is now up for sale again. It is structurally in superb order, and inside I was struck by the spacious rooms and by the magnificent plaster ceilings encircled by flower garlands and Scudamore coronets. More surprising was the huge ballroom with its arcaded *galerie des glaces* along one side. Outside, however, slumbers a great formal garden of the baroque age. The splendours of Hampton Court were recorded in superb topographical paintings, but north of Hereford no one bothered to depict what must have been laid out as its rival. How I longed to take a spade and uncover one of the flights of steps leading from one parterre to the next, which clearly lurked beneath the verdant slopes.

I recalled the earliest description of the garden, a century after its creation: 'all in King William's style of fortifications, surrounded by yew hedges, cut in a variety of forms, according to the taste of the times'. Holme Lacy is clearly a garden of great importance. Perhaps some day someone will wake it from its slumbers.

A Voice From the Past

NOT long after I wrote of Holme Lacy a letter came from Australia. Betty Urswick's grandfather had purchased the house in the years before the deluge of 1914. The *galerie des glaces* had been built for the coming-out dance for her and her cousin, an event which never took place. No one could have anticipated that war or its toll. All three of her grandfather's sons fell on the field of battle, and he himself died, too, during the course of the war.

Her grandparents and her aunts lie buried in the little church hard by. 'Perhaps if you go there again,' she wrote, 'you may see two little boys fishing in the Wye, and a very small girl pushing her doll's pram in the broad walk which ran from the house to the walled kitchen garden between the elephant yews.' Indeed, perhaps I might.

Last Facelift?

AFTER twenty years in a house, even its inmates realize that fashion has moved on, and that the papers and paint look a little weary. Despite a facelift into the 1980s, most of our rooms look tired, and we have had to steel ourselves for the dislocation that their redecoration involves.

Furniture, books, pictures, objects and the contents of cupboards are shunted around in piles from room to room, and one is made to realize the fragility of interior decoration both as an art form and as an expression of human personality. The hanging of a picture, the placing of a piece of porcelain to be shown to its best advantage or to stir memory, vanishes in a twinkling.

Suddenly, too, one realizes that this is probably the last time that a particular room will be changed within one's own lifetime. The choice of each wallpaper with mortality in mind makes it poignant. One stares at the samples pinned up on the walls of each room with a certain sense of finality that that will probably be it.

'MR CANCER'

∽∽∽

THE last time we were in Italy we traipsed the streets of Rome looking for a seed shop selling a salad mix which my wife always referred to as 'Mr Cancer'. It always struck me as rather an odd name, but it was not for me to question why, and inevitably I was never able to find it. At last in one florists', my wife said, 'Here it is,' picking up a packet that I had discarded. The label on it read 'La misticanza'. All was explained.

But what a deadly lack of imagination seizes the British when it comes to the ingredients of a green salad. John Evelyn would be horrified if he returned and saw what was available in most supermarkets: watery iceberg lettuces, that awful floppy greenhouse variety, and the terrible Chinese leaves. Evelyn's list for 'salletts' covering every month of the year is something that my wife, who runs the kitchen garden, tries to emulate. To achieve this, it has become essential to buy the odd packet of seeds abroad. And 'La misticanza' was a great find, a packet of mixed salad greens from which we will continue to pick leaves until the really hard frosts come. Plucking leaves is a discovery in itself, as against the usual British yanking up of a whole plant, and it is wonderful to pick a variety of them in terms of taste, leaf shape and colour.

This year we have had an abundance of *arugola* or rocket, so much so that I found myself looking for recipes demanding more than just a few leaves. A chance visit to an Italian restaurant brought to our attention a delicious and easily made dish: a bed of rocket tossed in good green *olio crudo*, with Parma ham laid over it and topped with slivers of fresh Parmesan. At the moment I am coping with a heavy crop of 'Rouge de Verona' chicory, saved by the discovery of a most wonderful lasagne recipe.

HELP YOURSELF

∼∽

FEW things are more distressing in the country than the despoliation of our parish churches. I remember some years ago expressing my concern to a former incumbent about an Elizabethan brass which was just left on the walls of the ruined medieval church at Llanwarne in Herefordshire, a building abandoned due to floods when a new church was built on a hill above it in the late-Victorian period. Untouched it may have been for about a century, but in the changed atmosphere of the late 1970s the brass went.

A similar flare went up over a Jacobean communion table which stood by the door at the back of Much Birch church, used as a handy repository for hymn and prayer books. One day that went, too. At the tiny church of Llandinabo, part of the same group, the candlesticks disappeared more than once over the years. Prudently, they are now taken in for the service and removed afterwards.

Good housekeeping is an essential part of running any church, and it is sad how often that attribute is missing. In that respect, what a splendid task the various branches of the National Association of Decorative and Fine Arts Societies – or NADFAS as we all know it – have done over the years in the way of compiling church inventories. In our group of churches I can report a happy ending to the saga of vanishing items. A few weeks back, when I pointed out that it was asking for trouble to leave a carved font bowl loose in the church porch, it was moved to safe keeping.

These are the experiences of just one person in a relatively remote part of England, the Welsh borderland of Herefordshire. What the overall picture must be, countrywide, I shudder to think. And at present there seems to be little on the horizon to suggest a reversal. Rather the contrary.

END OF AN ERA

WE motored up to stay with friends in Northumberland, hard by the Cheviots – which we never saw, as the mist held firm for the entire weekend. But it is glorious countryside, monumental in scale, like ours in Herefordshire but much emptier. Although I had gone there a number of times in the 1970s, my wife had not returned since 1939, when she was nine. Then her parents had taken a house at Bamburgh, and they had driven around looking at castles and churches and, of course, had gone to the seashore.

Our friends drove us on a sentimental journey to recall that holiday of half a century ago, and we walked along the beach near Craster, looking out to sea, picking up shells and tossing them into a plastic bag as contributions towards our grotto. In the distance, silhouetted against the horizon, arose the ruins of Dunstanburgh Castle.

Julia's previous visit had been at the end of August 1939. Every day had brought terrible news of the imminence of war and fear of an immediate invasion. Those days crystallized for her the end of an era. My father-in-law travelled south by train to do he knew not what. My mother-in-law gathered her young family into her car and sped south to her sister in Berkshire. Nothing was ever to be the same again.

INGENIOUSLY KNOTTED

∽∽∾

I HAVE an aversion to killing any living thing, but the two plump woodpigeons that waddle beneath my writing room window and savage the newly planted knots have rapidly succeeded in eroding my peaceful instincts. The interesting thing about knot garden recreations is that no two of them, even if derived from the same pattern, ever look identical. I had never meant to embark on these, but I had a lot of box left over and my mind turned towards the fulfilment of a dream of looking down onto a knot in front of the house. When we first came, I had planted six *Juniperus communis* 'Hibernica', stretching away from the front door across the lawn to a shrubbery and our ancient cedar. So our gardeners skimmed off the turf between the trees, making two twelve-foot squares.

The next stage was to find a design, not easy because all the old woodcut ones are so incredibly complex. However, in John Marriott's *Knots for Gardens* (1618), I came across the only simple one, rather more gothic than renaissance in form, with a lovely interlaced quatrefoil as its dominant motif. I found that to plant it I had to do exactly what Marriott's diagrams indicated – that is, peg out with string the two areas into a grid system crossed by diagonals. Then I started planting.

It is, I discovered, tremendously useful to draw out the design in bonemeal, which I dug in as I went along. Even then it is not easy. One's wellington boots get tied up in the string and, of course, the cat appears and thinks

the whole exercise is for his enjoyment. What struck me was the enormous concentration required to get it right, and it left me with a deep sense of the genius of those early gardeners who were able to plant huge knots, and many of them, with plants which required renewing every few years.

For the second knot I used the same pattern, but reversed the use of the two kinds of box, and being by then an old hand, I fairly whizzed along. Tiny though the plants are, I can see the pattern from my first-floor window and know the years of pleasure to come as I see it grow and mature into my old age.

A LINK WITH ELGAR

∞

LIFE in the country is always made up of figures in a landscape, some of whom embody part of it to the community around them. The passing of such a figure is always poignant and an occasion for reflection.

Sir Edward Elgar has meant much to us ever since the late Sir Frederick Ashton choreographed the ballet for which my wife provided both the idea and the design, *Enigma Variations*. It gave us joy to know that the house we bought had been visited by Elgar, although someone naughtily said that he chased the maids!

We mourned the passing of our elms, for they were the landscape he knew and loved. And we felt that another link had gone when the widow of his organist, Sir Percy Hull, died. Molly Hull was over ninety, but was one of those rare people to whom age was an irrelevance, and with whom each encounter was a delight. She remained devoted to the 1662 Prayer Book, which we keep going in our tiny church, and on the occasion of her funeral the church was packed. Never had our organ sounded so majestic as it responded to the skills of the cathedral organist playing what Molly had asked for: some Bach, a piece by Peter Warlock, and one of the preludes from Elgar's *The Dream of Gerontius*.

Two loved hymns, a psalm, a few prayers and three readings, and it was all over. Standing outside the church in the fitful winter sunshine, I was reminded of a letter describing Ellen Terry's funeral: 'It was all flowers and happiness and Edward Gordon Craig was heard to remark: "We must have more days like this." ' I now know what he meant.

SIGNS OF THE TIMES

EVERYONE we know seems to be going vegetarian, another herald of the Green Decade to come, but we soldier on eating meat, albeit far less of it. Our supplier is in the Cotswolds, where we go two or three times a year to load the car with what I refer to as the 'corpses'. I suppose, if it is looked at in one light, there is something gruesome about a boot-load of dismembered, bloody limbs. It is not far off Hammer films and those sequences through which I firmly shut my eyes while my wife, who was in the business, cheerfully looks on and tells me that all I am seeing is a mixture of cosmetic film blood and a pound of offal from the local butcher's, not a hatcheted human being.

Signs of the times always interest me, and as I was waiting for the order to be loaded the other day, a man came into the shop and began asking what was available which had no added preservatives. The man behind the counter was somewhat taken aback, and proceeded to seek advice from a colleague as to what did and what did not contain preservative, and in what quantity it figured in the range of delicious sausages they sell. What fascinated me was the customer, who was not, as one might have expected, long-haired, sandal-wearing and homespun, but a tweed-clad Mr Average shopping for the family.

BRIEF ENCOUNTERS

∽∽

I HAD not been to Cornwall for a couple of years, but I had agreed to give a lecture to help the Truro museum appeal. The energy and loyalty of local people never cease to amaze me. The intrepid organizer of the event, who had never done anything like this before, asked me how she should go about it. Always a believer in do it with style or not at all, I said: 'Get a lavish copper-plate invitation card printed, offer them only smoked salmon and champagne, and soak them for all you can.'

Well, in fact, the audience got jolly good value for their money, and twigged that this was to be a party. I stood peering down from the gallery of the museum, watching them arrive, and they were all dressed for an occasion. That was a splendid start, and from then on we did not look back. I never sensed that people had been cornered into having to come to some ghastly evening, and the party after the lecture was a real one.

One is always struck, when doing such events around the country, by how figures from one's past, or people who have read or been influenced by something one has said or done, step out of the audience afterwards. That is always touching Suddenly, things are said in retrospect that could never have been said at the time. The removal of the earlier context produces a brief and intense liberation. And in such encounters, knowing that the likelihood of ever meeting again is remote, a meeting of mind and spirit takes place in a few fleeting but memorable moments.

WASTE NOT . . .

MY wife always chides me if I cut the string from a parcel. I suppose it is a wartime upbringing that makes one conscious that in the running of a house, economy should be at the top of the list of priorities. Anything that can be re-used should be carefully packed away and stored against the day. And now is just the time to put such things into working order.

The old basket that hangs on a wooden peg near the door to the garden contains the string that has been carefully untied from many a parcel and then rewound for future use. Rubber bands that hold the post together are put into a container on a shelf in the kitchen, handy to wind around any recalcitrant screwtop bottle or jar.

Plastic margarine and ice-cream containers are sorted into sizes, stacked and placed in cardboard boxes clearly labelled on the sides, ready for action when the deep-freezing of summer fruits begins. Clear white wine bottles are taken down to the cellar awaiting use in the autumn for apple juice. Screw-top jars are sorted out and ranked in serried rows according to type and size in preparation for the coming season's chutney, pickles, and spiced fruits.

To enter the spring and summer months without all these things in good order is just as bad as having one's library all over the place.

EDWIN SMITH REMEMBERED

GOING along my bookshelves the other day, I stumbled across a number of books with photographs by Edwin Smith. They reminded me that it was his work which had inspired me just as much as the watercolours of John Piper, with a love of things English. In the 1950s and early 60s we were still in the pre-colour-plate age. Colour, when it was used, was generally confined to the dust jacket of a book with only, at best, a rarefied sprinkling within. This was the era of the photogravure plate, and what a master of this art Smith was. As a medium, its matt finish responded ideally to his orchestration of light, for Edwin Smith seemed able to bestow a magic aureole onto everything upon which he turned his lens.

He was active in the post-war period, when country houses were only just tentatively swinging wide their doors to the public, and most still retained their mystery. All those years ago, it was his pictures that opened my eyes, giving me, a child of the terraced London suburbs, my first glimpses of a world I knew not, one of village, cottage, church and manor house.

The pictures are unashamedly romantic, revelling in reflections and a sense of having penetrated the Sleeping Beauty's palace through a melancholy tangle of branches and leaves, ivy and lichen. Smith loved strong, grainy contrast, and some of the skies are heavy, laden with threatening clouds, which add drama to the scene below. No picture was just an illustration, nor merely an *aide-memoire*, but purveyed a poetic vision of England in the aftermath of a war whose consequences threatened the very survival of everything he photographed.

Images have enormous power, far more than words, and this is particularly the case for people of an aesthetic cast of mind. Those brought up on these pictures were to form the generation which spearheaded the fight for the English heritage in the 1970s and beyond. With these thoughts I placed the books back on the shelf with reverence and gratitude.

A FORGOTTEN CAPITAL

LUDLOW always casts its spell over me. I first visited the town thirty years ago for a matinée of Milton's *Comus* performed in the castle whose great hall had been the setting for its first performance. Never could Sabrina have arisen from her 'glassy, cool translucent wave' more magically than when she stepped up from behind what was a simple platform.

Working on a radio programme recently, made me pace Ludlow's streets and look at it more closely than ever before. Nowhere else can the experience of pre-Civil War urban life be more vividly recaptured: the interplay between town and country glimpsed at every turn, each street giving way quickly to landscape, a hill town held in by a verdure tapestry. And they are streets still lived in, just as in the age of the great Elizabeth and of the first two Stuarts.

Its life today resembles that of an Oxford college more than that of a late twentieth-century town. Everyone seems to know everyone. And, oh, what houses lurk behind those façades, often merely a Georgian red-brick skin giving the face of fashion to medieval or Tudor timber, lathe and plaster. And hidden gardens, too. No wonder the Ludlow Research Group is charting the architectural and social history of every building.

Ludlow is a treasure house which, mercifully, never gave birth to a Shakespeare to ruin it. Those who live there guard it as a precious jewel. And rightly so. I always have to remind myself that I am strolling through what was the capital of Wales for a century and a half. Who would think that this overgrown village was once a capital city, let alone an oasis of Renaissance civilization on the Welsh Borders. And yet one only has to look, for instance, at one tomb in the church to know the truth of it, for here lies Philip Sidney's sister Ambrosia, a young

Juliet gathered at fourteen, in a monument which is a trumpet salute to all that had happened in distant Italy.

As the daylight fades on a cold winter's day, the mind's eye finds little difficulty in peopling its streets with cavalcades of querulous Welsh come to fight it out in court, bustling officials and lawyers in feathered bonnets, bristling ruffs and muffled cloaks, and the townspeople in their honest woollens plying their wares in the market square that is still in use today. If only we had had an English Avercamp to paint the scene.

BOOK CITY

IF Ludlow is one hilltop town within striking distance of home, Hay-on-Wye is another. We drove there one December day when the hills encircling it dissolved into the rainclouds. The landscape could have been lifted out of a hunting piece by John Wootton. Hay was never grand, although it, too, has a castle presiding over the few streets gathered beneath its walls.

More than twenty years ago, when we first came to live in this part of the country, going to Hay was like a journey on a time machine back to the 1930s, and we rushed to buy sepia postcards in shops whose windows were arranged in pre-war style.

Today, these shops seem to have moved on to the 1950s; but the biggest change is that Hay has become book city, the world's largest dumping ground for second-hand books. On the whole, that has not proved a cruel fate. On its narrow pavements, sturdy Welsh locals jostle with the exotic youth dropped out from Thatcher's England – a decorative motley crew in a raggle-taggle of fabric and colour, serving in the bookshops and propping up the healthfood, craft and antique shops. The contrast with Ludlow only a few miles away could hardly be more striking.

WINTER PRUNING

THE gargantuan and seemingly never-ending winter pruning is well under way. We really should purchase a small rolling gantry before I fall off the light metal-alloy ladder on top of which I balance, pruning with my right hand while my left clutches hard onto anything in proximity. Most of the time is spent trying to site the wretched ladder on ground riddled by mole tunnels, down which one leg or another has been known to collapse, jerking the steps and me with them at a pre-cipitous angle.

The pleached lime avenue has already been done. I soldiered along its triple tier during late November, noting with some satisfaction that there are now few parts of it where the lateral branches do not meet and intertwine. The growth always astonishes me: shoots three feet to four feet in length in a single year. I feel a little sad to be removing them, as their incandescent fiery red is glorious in winter sunshine. I wish that I could be as organized as Rosemary Verey at Barnsley, who leaves the top layer of shoots till later, just to enjoy the beauty of that magic forest of crimson twigs bursting across the skyline. But once I am on that ladder it is then or not at all.

At the moment Wilf is pruning the amelanchiers in the rose garden, according to what Graham Rose, the garden writer, dubbed Strong's law. Four trees stand in the spandrels formed by the box-edged beds, but, alas, one grew little because its roots soon hit rock. Some years back, the lack of balance in the composition became only too apparent, and for the first time I cut back the other three to the size of the one whose growth was sluggish, thereby enacting my law.

Farewell To Muff

∞∞∞

THE Reverend Wenceslas Muff is no more. All those who have lost a greatly loved creature whose every movement was entwined into their lives will know the sense of grief and desolation.

We had not heard of cat AIDS, but it is apparently rampant in Herefordshire, communicated usually by a bite from a feral cat. The effect is the same as the human variety, the brain and intellect still there, but housed within a disintegrating physical system. The result was a life cut short.

He lies buried with his toys in a secluded corner at the foot of a clipped yew with a crown on its summit, at the end of his favourite walk. His monument is in the making, a golden ball atop a pedestal, into the four panels of which will be set inscriptions in gold on slate, two celebrating his greatest attributes: 'Loving' and

'Brave'. For more than a decade he was the spirit of the place, filling every corner with his green eyes and bushy black tail.

But life must go on, and we now have the joy of two new kittens, William Larkin Esq and Herzog Friedrich von Sans Souci: odd ways to commemorate finishing a book on a Jacobean painter and a visit to Potsdam.

It is the first time that we have had cats which are not moggies, for these are Maine Coons, a breed of long-haired cat which, when fully grown, can reach up to twenty pounds in weight. They come from New England where they used to be sturdy farmyard cats in the last century, some say descended from those delectable felines one sees being hugged in pastels by Perroneau.

They come from a herbaceous family, with a father called Basil and mothers Poppy and Rosemary, and with the curious double relationship of being uncle and nephew and half-brothers at one and the same time. One is a silver tabby and the other is tabby with white markings.

An odd trait is that they can flick the water out of their bowl over the kitchen floor. This goes back to having to break the ice for water in the cold winters of Maine. The other trait is a short-cut to human enslavement, for they love staring their owners in the eye.

THE FLOOD

FOR more than a week, Ross-on-Wye has looked like the Venice of Hereford, or perhaps the Mont St Michel. It is engulfed in the worst flood waters for decades. The road leading to the town seems to cross a vast lagoon out of which protrude branches of trees, the roofs of barns and, more incongruously, the tops of goalposts of the local playing-field. In one sense it looks beautiful to see the picturesque town centre with its soaring steeple reflected in the waters.

We have been awash as never before, with dull, leaden skies pouring rain down, often as long as thirty-six hours at a stretch without ceasing. Our lane, descending to the village of Hoarwithy, on the Wye, was never without a stream or a minor cascade. In the old days the council used to ditch, but no longer. Instead of culverts and ditches forming a continuous drainage system leading down to the river, the water is forced to gush and flow where it will.

At Hoarwithy it was up to the arch of the bridge, and lapping close to the riverside inn. One approach to Hereford itself was closed for a period.

Now is the time for planting, but what hope! Every hole dug merely fills up with water. 'February fill dyke', so the old saying goes. The seasons at the moment seem all awry.

History Lesson

∾⌘⌘∾

WHEN reading about the Civil War recently, one single fact haunted my mind. More families were affected by losses in that conflict than during the First World War. It brought home to me, for the first time, just how savage the Civil War must have been. Out of twenty-one men who went from the Shropshire village of Myddle, for example, only nine returned. Can one imagine anything more heart-rending? For it was a war in which like fought like, in which whole families and communities were rent asunder.

Even today, one hardly has to travel any distance to

find evidence of the cataclysm still visible on the landscape. Only a short drive away from here rise the noble
ruins of Raglan Castle, the seat of the Marquesses of
Worcester, on the Welsh Marches. Raglan Castle was
the last royalist stronghold to fall, after a devastating
siege. Then its splendours were given over to the pick-
axes and pillage of the rabble who, in a short time,
managed to destroy for ever an outpost of civilization.
How unutterably awful it must have been to see that
happen.

No wonder that the Civil War left such a legacy of
fear in the English mind, and no wonder one still tends
to recall it whenever society shows signs of polarizing
sharply.

CHRISTMAS DECORATIONS

THE Christmas decorations live in the drawers of an
ebony cabinet awaiting their annual exposition, a bit like
relics, for that indeed is almost what many of them have
become. Out they come, memories of past Christmases
without number, stretching back to the late Victorian
period, frail remnants of the festive season as celebrated
by one family in peace as well as in war, and in several
different places.

One cardboard box is labelled somewhat strangely
'Christmas Decorations and Gold Fish Bowl Animals'.
Carefully laid to rest in swathes of cotton wool, the old
glass decorations nestle, faded red ribbons attached to
their rings for tying them to a tree we never have,

preferring instead to pile them into bowls as table centres or attach them to the excrescences of wall brackets around the house. Even when they are broken the decorations are still left to lie there, reflections of a fear of discarding a single distant memory.

The collection is added to over the years, usually with American purchases, for there the Germanic and Scandinavian tradition of Christmas mingles with a sense of good taste which we seem to lack. So now, added to pre-war glitter is an overlay of baroque angels with stiffened, fluttering robes, wreaths of snow-clad fir cones and translucent glass crystals. And, like their predecessors, they, too, each silly item of them, have become the embodiment of sentiment and memory.

TABLESCAPES

∞∞

PERHAPS at no other time of year is so much thought given to that most ephemeral of arts, table-laying. Even the most aesthetically dead seem able to rally and place something on the table, if only a candle wreathed in plastic holly. Christmas and New Year present a succession of occasions for lingering at the table, and not just putting in an appearance for the necessity of food. Everyone senses that there is time to look at and appreciate every detail, unusual in an age when it seems that the family together at table is an exception rather than a norm of life.

We have always had a slightly eighteenth-century approach to eating, in that we move from room to room

– three in all. Blue and white china gives way to Victorian prints, and they, in turn, to family portraits. Each background sets its own mood, but it is the mutations on the table's surface over the festive season that give the most delight.

Every shade and pattern of tablecloth and napkin, every service, however debilitated, every piece of silver and table decoration, are orchestrated in succession. There is also time to contemplate the composition of each tableau, and, if guests are to come, to consider the theatrical impact of leading them in when the candles are lit and the flames flicker, bringing the glitter and sparkle to life.

Strong reds and greens can be used for these celebratory gatherings in a way which would be totally out of place for the rest of the year. So one fumbles to the bottom of the drawer of table linen, looking for those once-a-year cloths and napkins.

It is the improvisation of it all that holds the strongest appeal: a horrendous green tablecloth being transformed into something of beauty by throwing cascades of lace over it; the dull epergne which springs to life when piled high with sweets in gold or silver metallic paper; or the satisfaction of cobbling a wintry arcadia from the disparate pile of holly, mistletoe and twigs from the garden.

MEMORY HOLD THE DOOR

CHRISTMAS is Janus-faced. One side is joy, the other grief. It opens gates of memory firmly locked into a corner of the mind for the rest of the year. But when the festive season beckons, those gates open and the past comes back to take us in its embrace. Christmas is always as much about those not there as about those present. The card no longer received because the sender is no more, the telephone which does not ring this year to remind us of a friendship around the globe, the person who is not at the table, the visit which is no longer made.

But then the sadness fades, for that gate lets in not only tears of grief but those of joy, and thankfulness, too. Memory's sacred role is to hold in the mind all those whom one has loved. At Christmas they come tumbling back in a season when recollection pulls strongly on the emotions. How often over these days leading into the New Year does the conversation harken back to times past, to people and events long since gone. Too many sentences to my wife seem to begin with, 'Do you remember?' A smile crosses the face, maybe the eyes water just a little, and a silence follows, for nothing more needs to be said where the mutual understanding is so perfect.

Always the twelve days of Christmas take on the character of a garland of friendships through time, for not only those of yesterday are recalled, but those of today rekindled. We are reminded of their centrality in any life. Age and bad times make them a bedrock, giving us the strength to go forward into whatever the new year will bring.

Dog Days

~∞∞~

ALTHOUGH the shortest day is over, these are dog days for life in the country. The good company of Christmas has gone and the earliest spring bulbs have yet to show their petals. This is the time of year to stay in, comforted by the fragrance of bowls of pink and white hyacinths promising joys to come. All that is needed from the outside world on most days, and certainly in bad weather, is concentrated into one major expedition undertaken before darkness falls.

It is always a struggle. Emerging like a Brueghel peasant, one has to take in the state of the fuel, check the oil supply, collect the newspapers left in a box in an outhouse, harvest what vegetables and salad stuff are needed for the kitchen, without forgetting the herbs. As the cook, I recall the look of valiant resignation which overcomes my wife when, halfway through a recipe, I ask for a sprig of this or that, when it is pitch black outside or even worse. I must say, however, that there are few times when she has not risen to the occasion.

New Year Spangles

As I write this, I look out on a garden bespangled with frost, for all the world like one of those winter transformation scenes in a pantomime, which I adored as a child and tried to recreate in my toy theatre. Spangled is a lovely word, much used by the Elizabethans in respect of their clothes, and that is exactly what I see.

Blue sky and bright sunlight fall across the frost-laden branches of the great cedar tree we fell in love with when we bought the house nearly two decades ago. Flora, nestling below, seems to clutch her hoary basket of fruits and flowers closer to her, as though to protect them, and the knot gardens over which she presides are etched in silver. I know of few more ravishing winter sights to carry me with happiness into the unknown of a new year.

Angels With Claws

Our American Maine Coons have settled in very quickly. Cats easily recognize the feline-fixated, and these 'angels', as A. L. Rowse dubbed them, have the household revolving round them already. We would not have it any other way. I am not sure that I would not add the word 'fallen' to his apt description, as we are now the poorer by a handsome blue and white plate.

Having never before watched kittens grow up, we have been astonished how soon their characters develop.

Larkin, like John Betjeman, is in love with being a geriatric, at eight months a dignified silvery old gentleman with a stately gait. He is most affectionate, sitting looking up at me with a smile, asking to be gathered up and cuddled. Souci is smaller in build, and not for nothing called 'that wicked Souci', for he is into everything, and when told firmly not to do something, always answers back. But he is equally loving, hurtling himself into my lap.

Until recently they lived in the house, with access to a large wire pen outdoors for air and exercise, but now the big decision has to be made, whether to let them roam on their own. After the fate of their predecessor, there lingers a reluctance.

TIME PIECES

❧

ANY house in the country runs on diaries and calendars, and January is a month which makes me acutely aware of that fact. On the breakfast table is my new *Cats in Art* diary. Having transcribed from last year's diary when certain things in the garden have to be done, into the bookshelf the old one goes. Then, as the year proceeds, each day I note the weather, what is happening in the garden, and, in brackets, what I have achieved in my writing room.

My wife sits opposite me, also filling one in. We do not look at each other's diaries, but I am keenly aware from stray remarks that into hers goes everything from notes on oil deliveries and servicing the Aga to the quantities of preserves and fruit juice she produces.

In the kitchen hangs perhaps the most crucial diary of the lot: the teddy bear calendar over the telephone. By long tradition I buy my wife this irresistible piece of nonsense each Christmas, and we stick to not revealing the next month's bear tableau until we have reached the day. January's has an old and a young bear wrapped in cosy scarfs, looking at the night sky through a telescope – a composition with Epiphany in mind, I suppose.

The stars would certainly be easier to read than the hieroglyphics on the sheet of days in the month below. Onto it goes, in a letters and numbers system of our own invention, all the comings and goings and events associated with running the house.

A LONG-LIVED CAKE

ALTHOUGH we have a policy of putting Christmas 'to bed' as soon after New Year's Day as possible, one element has a habit of lingering on until the end of January: the cake. No other comestible in the year endures such a prolonged consumption, or indeed pre-history. The Christmas cake usually starts its life in late November – first made, then engulfed in marzipan, icing and decorations, before being tinned, to await the great day. Thereafter, it does not seem to matter how many slices are taken from it; when the tin is opened, there it is still looking up at me.

There is always a sadness to slicing a Christmas cake for it is defacing an art work. 'Happy Christmas' in vivid pink soon becomes an indecipherable message. One by one, Santa Claus, sprigs of artificial holly and fir trees are uprooted from the marzipan. I am always glad when it is gone, for there is nothing quite so gloomy as living with the ghost of Christmas past.

HYACINTH VASES

EVEN if, outside, spring seems sadly all too far off, within there is the comfort of bowls and glasses filled with hyacinths. These my wife has carefully nurtured in the dark, awaiting the moment for their epiphany in the living room of the house. The intent has always been to have the atmosphere of the festive season heavy with

their fragrance, but we have never succeeded in achieving that. The glass hyacinth vases are a story in themselves, being difficult to find. We lighted upon some once along that marvellous part of the *quais* in Paris, which is an explosion of things horticultural. More surprising was the group I snapped up outside a filling station in Oxford.

Now they stand dotted around on the breakfast table, in the hall and in the drawing room, their flowerheads just shyly thrusting upwards through the tender spikes of green leaves. Within the house they give us the earliest flower tints of the new year, the slightest glimpse of which, on the greyest of days, lifts the spirits: the pure paper white of 'L'Innocence', the Edwardian pink of 'Lady Derby', and the soft, pale yellow of 'City of Haarlem'. Bowls are filled with the bouquets of the miniature pink 'Rosalie' and blue 'Borah'. As the American Christmas pot pourri of pine cones, scented woods and berries fades, the air fills with a fragrance which promises what is to come in the garden.

THE GREAT HURRICANE

25 JANUARY 1990 will go down in the annals of our house as the day of the great hurricane. We missed the really mighty one in 1987, which came nowhere near the Welsh borders, but this time we were not so lucky. Idiotically, as the day progressed, we rather thought that we were to be twice blessed.

After a nightmare drive from London, taking eight as

against the usual three hours, we entered Herefordshire, noting that there seemed few signs of wind damage, but by then it was pitch dark. Indeed, calm reigned as we travelled the last lap of road from Ross-on-Wye, then down the lane to the house and up the drive. Suddenly, however, the headlamps hit the massive trunk of our old Scots pine which had come down right across the drive. We had to climb over it to get into the house.

We had a sentiment about that tree which we owed to my late father-in-law who, on first coming to the house, remarked, 'Oh, you've got a Charlie tree', referring to the old country tradition that a Scots pine was always planted by Jacobites to indicate to the Young Pretender that it was a safe house. Of course, ours cannot have been much more than a century old, but there it lay, a piece of history gone, and yet another casualty in the long list of mature trees that we have laid to rest in our grounds during the last two decades.

As in all such dramas, there were blessings to be counted. It had not crashed through the front of the house, and although it had annihilated a section of old thuya hedging, and had fallen across the front lawn, the newly planted Jacobean knots and six ten-foot-high junipers had survived undamaged.

Far sadder, in our mnenomic garden, was the savaging of most of what we call Calista's tree, a crataegus named after an American friend who gave it to us when she stayed here years ago. My wife had just sent her pictures of its glowing red fruits on the bough in midwinter. With our friend's seventieth birthday only a few days away, my wife and I decided to commemorate it with a new tree.

He Also Serves . . .

∾

WHY are we waiting? Is this a feature of daily life only for those who live in the country? Why is it that waiting about for this or that so nags the mind – somehow it always seems to end up ruining the day. Lately, we have been plagued by people who do not turn up. In the country, times assigned for turning up are rarely more specific than morning or afternoon.

I rang up the plumber the other day, asking him to come and deal with a blocked drain. Yes: he would come tomorrow – Friday. We stay in. He fails to materialize. On Monday, I ring him. Oh, he did come, but it was on Saturday and we were not there. Exuding charm through clenched teeth, I manage to persuade him to come tomorrow. No problem he says: he'll be there. We are still waiting.

My feeling of annoyance was exacerbated by a saga over the despatch of a new photocopier, which was always going to be delivered, definitely by ten o'clock in the morning, on a series of successive days. At the moment, we are steadying our nerves for a promised 'immediate' delivery of snowdrops in the green. I wonder.

It is the decimation of the mind that I most resent, the ravishment of order, punctuality, good time-keeping, prompt service and the meeting of deadlines – all those things round which my own life has always revolved. For those who flaunt such things, who do not come or fail to deliver, there must, I conclude, be a different construct of psyche. It must be devoid of any sense of remorse or guilt, or indeed any notion that apology exists, even as an idea. And yet these people survive and flourish. I find myself wondering whether I am just old-fashioned, and if my life would be easier if I joined them.

AWAY FROM IT ALL

I HAVE been in the country virtually the whole time since Christmas – a long stretch without the wicked city. January and February are pretty awful months, ones in which the weather enhances the sense of enclosure and isolation, which not even papers, television or radio quite eradicate.

Suddenly, I am acutely aware of a kinship with the England of Jane Austen, in which the fashionable chatter of the metropolis percolates only fitfully with the backdrop of a war on the mainland of Europe, while civilized life in the country still goes on. *Plus ça change . . .*

DOOKS MARMALADE

JANUARY is marmalade-making time, as the first Seville oranges appear in Hereford market or the local super-store. For a week the kitchen, scullery and adjacent offices are made over to a bewildering array of preserving pans, suspended muslin sieves, a huge stoneware bowl, piles of fruit, stacks of weighed sugar, and an array of glass jars exhumed from the cellar. The atmosphere is perfumed with the pungent aromatic scent of oranges.

The handling of the fruit is quite another matter, for after squeezing mounds of them, and cutting the peel up, I enter the Lady Macbeth syndrome, forever washing my

hands and praying that the 'damned spot', the smell, would go. Preserves and all forms of bottling are my wife's domain, and she always makes at least three varieties of marmalade, of which by far the best is a rich, dark confection taking several days to make, and known as Dooks Marmalade.

Dooks was the nickname of my late mother-in-law's nanny. She it was who brought up the large family of Sir Ernest Trevelyan after the death of his second wife in her very early forties. The children all adored Dooks, and her love for them was so great that she concealed from her charges the fact that she had married. It was years before she was caught, by accident, wearing her wedding ring. But the secret was kept until the children were old enough to make the adjustment, and in gratitude they bought her and her husband a small farm.

So, every year, when my wife follows the recipe written out in her mother's early-in-the-century hand, the tale is retold of the sacrifice of one dedicated woman in the Oxford of Zuleika Dobson. How surprised she would be to open our store cupboard and find the neat rows of jars with their deep amber content, all bearing her name, 'Dooks Marmalade'.

SCRAPBOOKS

෴

WE continue to mount our scrapbooks throughout the year, but in the depths of winter that task becomes a special pleasure. Every day after lunch we adjourn for twenty minutes to a small room where a table is set up with books, scissors and guillotine, glue, packets of photos and files of other materials, newspaper cuttings, invitation cards, restaurant and hotel cards, entry tickets. Everything has to be sorted and filed under month and date.

It is in winter particularly that the time delay in keeping up with all this works to magical advantage. Because we usually happen to be between three and four months behind, we are probably busy pasting up material from, say, a tour of north Portugal, and the sunshine which is missing outside is pouring across the pages, each group of material recalling some fresh delight in terms of pictures and landscape, buildings and people.

We are both avid collectors of every form of ephemeral memory-prompter, snapping every hotel room, however drear, restaurants and meals, forms of transportation, the view from the bedroom window, the railway station, the bar . . .

BULB BONUS

BULB suppliers can be notoriously unreliable. A friend sent us a number of *Sternbergia lutea*, lovely autumn-flowering plants with buttercup-yellow flowers. They were sent to remind us of a visit to Ninfa, near Sermoneta, south of Rome. That romantic garden, with its magical wild profusion of planting amid the ruined walls of an early medieval town was carpeted with them at the time.

My wife carefully sited this little group in what she

calls her Scandinavian grove, a triangle of land wedged between formal areas, from which silver birch trees soar upwards but between which she has created a wild planting like a verdure tapestry. Much to our surprise, the flowers appeared in winter – and white instead of yellow.

Rushing to the illustrated plant directories, and then to our catalogues of bulb suppliers, we found ourselves the proud possessors of a much rarer, and indeed more expensive bulb, *Sternbergia candida*. We seem to have benefited handsomely from the mistake.

WALKING THE CAT

THE decision had been reached that our Maine Coon cats were not to roam. As a result, the great adventure has been breaking Larkin and Souci into the routine of a daily walk. Souci has a bright blue harness and Larkin a black one, and after some initial difficulties, we can now put on these without a major drama. Everything has settled down to a ritual. At about five o'clock, a tin full of cat 'bickies' is rattled, effecting the pair's instant appearance in the kitchen from the remotest corners of the house. Seven tiny cat biscuits are counted out carefully for each cat. This, they know, is the signal for their harnesses to be put on, and they either sit in keen anticipation or perversely vanish beneath a table.

From the outset, their attitudes to these expeditions have been different. Souci is the Tarzan of the two, having only to see something vertical to go up it, which leads to tremendous tussles to get him down. He parades rather than walks, his eyes set keenly ahead, occasionally emitting a delicious chirrup of delight. Larkin climbs only occasionally, but often sits at the bottom of a tree, thinking he ought to climb it to prove his felinity. On the whole, he likes to concentrate on a constricted area, examining it with Sherlock Holmes-like intensity. If I attempt to move him on he refuses to budge, and I am rewarded with a sinister growl.

Souci, however, now knows what to do when one says 'Home, home', and instantly rushes across the garden to the pen at the back of the house, my wife hurtling along behind. Visitors who chance upon this picturesque spectacle of the walk are rightly amused and think of us as, perhaps, a little eccentric.

ROCOCO REVERIE

PICTURES in the papers of the gargantuan drifts of snowdrops at Painswick in Gloucestershire encouraged us to view the progress made on the Rococo Garden seven years on. The most remarkable feature was always the site, a small combe or valley around which a path serpentines, punctuated by buildings aligned to vistas, catching that moment in the eighteenth century when baroque formality was offset by the cult of the wiggly walk.

Huge advances in the restoration have been made in the intervening years, above all in reinstating the almost Disneyland gothic follies recorded in the watercolour panorama of the garden by Thomas Robins. From afar, as one sees them on entering the garden, they look like cake decorations. No concern for the hand of time here, with moss and lichen, but a case rather of all things bright and beautiful.

The so-called Eagle House is a sugar pink and white gothic gazebo, seemingly floating above the hillside. A great vista leads to a gothic exedra of wood and pasteboard, apparently cut out of white paper. It is the stimulation given to garden ideas for oneself which most excites, and I already have an itch for the paint pot this summer, bringing colour into the garden in a way we have largely forgotten.

But perhaps the most daring effect, alas too late for us to copy, is that this meandering tour looks down onto a geometric kitchen garden at its heart below. Now that would be something to emulate.

EPILOGUE

HOW can I end? In a sense I cannot, for my life in the country lies as much in the future as it does in the past. On re-reading these jottings, I am struck by my good fortune in ever having had such a period. They sing out to me how right I was, just past my half-century, to strike out in a new direction. They remind me that often life's most significant moments are made up of small, fleeting thoughts, emotions and responses set off by encounters with people, places and things, a memory recalled, the eye suddenly entranced, the past unexpectedly evoked or the spirits caught up on the wings of joy.

When I was asked to write my diary I did so with precisely these thoughts in mind. There is always room for a beam of light to remind us of the nobility and beauty of ordinary things, to celebrate them, but also to give thanks.

POSTSCRIPT

I T is now eight years on, but life continues at The Laskett unchanged. The kitchen still fills with the aroma of Dook's marmalade each January, our fish still comes from the stall in Ross market every Thursday, the Finnish apple steamer goes on the Aga each October, a motley collection of decorated eggs enlivens our Easter table as it has done for years . . . The simple, often silly, beauties of the domestic year, harbingers of continuity and memory, are re-enacted in an unending cycle, and yet no one can be wholly isolated from the world without. We were in the midst of Foot and Mouth and the cattle, sheep and lambs in the fields around were shot one sunlit spring afternoon. It was not one ever to be forgotten. But it is at moments like this that the small ordinary things become an anchor. Life has to go on even in the face of tragedy.

Our own greatest loss was beloved Larkin. We took him to the vet and never returned with him. A decision had to be taken and it is a day neither of us ever wish to re-live. It was all so unexpected, and we were so utterly unprepared. He rests now in the orchard beneath the grass through which on warm sunny days he loved to stroll and in which he would suddenly roll over in bliss. I miss him still. A monument has yet to come, but a large stone marks the spot and I place on it from time to time a sprig of rosemary. He is not forgotten. But Lettice, Lady Laskett has come, a beautiful tortoiseshell Maine Coon, who has enslaved us from the day of her arrival.

In the end her beguiling and sometimes impertinent ways brought Souci out of mourning. For that we are grateful.

I write this on an early autumn morning. I look out on a tapestry of leaves, still green, but dappled with an aureole of gold. Feathery sprigs of yew remind me of a hedge yet to be cut. In the orchard the plums are being harvested for compote for the winter. The apples still hang bright on the trees, beautiful in this light. In the borders the golds of late summer are being tempered already by the purples and violets of autumn. I hear the sound of trickling water from the fountain near the house and, in the foreground, the chirping of the house martins in the eaves just above my writing room window. I draw a happy breath as another day at The Laskett is about to begin. There's always so much to look forward to and also to be grateful for in that simple phrase, *At Home in the English Countryside*.

Roy Strong
The Laskett, 2002